COMBAT AIRCRAFT

130 B-58 HUSTLER UNITS

36
U.S. AIR FORCE

SERIES EDITOR TONY HOLMES

130 COMBAT AIRCRAFT

Peter E Davies

B-58 HUSTLER UNITS

OSPREY PUBLISHING

OSPREY PUBLISHING
Bloomsbury Publishing Plc
Kemp House, Chawley Park, Cumnor Hill, Oxford OX2 9PH, UK
29 Earlsfort Terrace, Dublin 2, Ireland
1385 Broadway, 5th Floor, New York, NY 10018, USA
Email: info@ospreypublishing.com
www.ospreypublishing.com

OSPREY is a trademark of Osprey Publishing Ltd

First published in Great Britain in 2019
Transferred to digital print in 2023

A catalogue record for this book is available from the British Library.

Print ISBN: 978 1 4728 3640 3
ePub: 978 1 4728 3641 0
ePDF: 978 1 4728 3642 7
XML: 978 1 4728 3643 4

Edited by Tony Holmes
Cover artwork by Gareth Hector
Aircraft profiles by Jim Laurier
Index by Angela Hall
Originated by PDQ Digital Media Solutions, UK
Printed and bound in India by Replika Press Private Ltd.

23 24 25 26 27 10 9 8 7 6 5 4 3

Acknowledgements
I am grateful to members of the B-58 Hustler Association, including Col Howard Bialas USAF (Ret), George A Haloulakos MBA, CFA, Dr Stan Moody and Capt David L Sharrock USAF (Ret). Thank you also to SSgts Neil Byrd USAF (Ret) and Ken Kimmons USAF (Ret), and to Terry Panopalis, Capt Josh Densmore USAF (Ret) and Jim Eastham for the provision of photographs.

Front Cover
In the 1950s it became increasingly clear that advances in Soviet ground-to-air missile development would make the USAF Strategic Air Command's preference for high-speed bombers attacking from high altitude unacceptably hazardous. Convair and the USAF decided to test the B-58 Hustler as a low-altitude penetrator, requiring all its equipment to function during the course of three flights at altitudes as low as 50 ft.

On 18 September 1958, RB-58 58-1015 (the 22nd Hustler off the production line and one of the initial test batch of 30 YB-58 development examples) was used for the third flight – a long distance, low altitude test. Crewed by Convair pilot B A Erickson, with J A Rogerson and A G Mitchell as navigator and flight engineer, respectively, the aircraft, christened *Little Joe*, took off from Carswell AFB, Texas, and flew for 1220 miles at an average speed of 610 knots at an altitude of 500 ft or less over the arid territory of west Texas, Arizona and southern California. On one section they skimmed over a slightly more fertile area of New Mexico below 200 ft at 700 mph to establish whether airborne bugs would obscure the pilot's visibility at that altitude. The windscreen's V-shape deflected this potential threat to safety, although there were no windscreen wipers – just a pneumatic system for high-pressure air. The flight included a simulated strike on Edwards AFB, an in-flight refuelling and an approach to a secondary 'target' at Vandenberg AFB, California, although this part of the mission was aborted due to fog. The whole flight, including the return leg at operational cruise altitude, was made visually using dead reckoning, and the jet covered 2069 miles in four hours and three minutes. The aircraft demonstrated pleasing stability and gust response throughout its simulated strike mission.

Just over a year later, 58-1015 made the type's first sustained Mach 2 flight, and it continued to serve as a test aircraft at Edwards AFB before conversion to service production standard and delivery to the 43rd BW in 1962 (*Cover artwork by Gareth Hector*)

PREVIOUS PAGES
B-58As were usually seen with underfuselage pods in place, but this 305th BW aircraft (59-2436) cruises in clean configuration in August 1969. Nine years earlier it had been the very first B-58A delivered to the 43rd BW with a full set of tactical systems in place. The varied metal tones of its unpainted exterior indicated the three types of honeycomb panels used – fibreglass, aluminium and stainless steel, the latter forming the rear sections of the engine nacelles (*Terry Panopalis*)

CONTENTS

CHAPTER ONE

DELTA DESIGN

Side-by-side seating was chosen for the two-seat 'Tub' version of the F-102A, with consequent degradation in airspeed. This TF-102A, assigned to the 497th Fighter Interceptor Squadron at Torrejon, Spain, performed the same pilot proficiency and transition training for Delta Dagger pilots that other identical examples would provide for B-58A Hustler pilots in the 1960s. Some single-seat F-102As were also supplied to SAC units for solo flight experience (*USAF*)

The Cold War engendered a frantic pace in defence technology as East and West strove to meet the real or imagined threats lurking in each others' armouries. This was most evident in the evolution of advanced aerial weapons systems, and the B-58A Hustler of the 1950s – the world's first supersonic bomber – was a prime example of America's colossal investment and technical success in staying ahead. It originated in 1949 only two years after Chuck Yeager had shown that manned supersonic flight was possible. His tiny single-seat Bell X-1 rocket aeroplane briefly exceeded Mach 1, but only two years later the USAF was seriously considering long-range sustained flight at Mach 2 using conventional turbojet power in a large bomber.

At that time there was no turbojet anywhere near powerful enough for the task, and very little relevant research information. Innovations such as swept-back wings, afterburning jet engines and ejection seats were still at early stages in their development, and knowledge of delta wings was largely confined to wind-tunnel studies of a captured German Lippisch DM-1 wooden glider – the first pure delta wing aircraft. It had a thick wing spanning 19 ft 8 in, with a leading edge sweep of 60 degrees. The ten-foot-tall tail fin was almost as long as the 20 ft 9 in fuselage, and it included the pilot's canopy.

The National Advisory Committee for Aeronautics (NACA) wind-tunnel tests revealed some serious shortcomings in terms of lift, drag and stability, and its designer, Alexander Lippisch, had already moved on in 1945 to experiment with more efficient designs such as his P-13 and P-14 that were to have been rocket-powered with the intention of reaching Mach 1.85. Lippisch had flown a Delta 1 glider in 1930, a powered version with a 30 hp Bristol Cherub engine shortly thereafter, and the DFS 194 rocket-powered delta, which, in 1937, was a direct progenitor of the Messerschmitt Me 163 interceptor.

The delta concept caught the attention of the Consolidated Vultee Aircraft Corporation, which was working on 1945 USAAF requests for proposals for a long-range escort fighter and a supersonic interceptor. The company won the interceptor contract in June 1946 and began work on two Model 7000 (XP-92) prototypes. Initially, the fighter used the currently-fashionable 35-degree swept wing combined with a V-tail and rocket power, although chief designer Adolph Burstein preferred a more radical approach and advocated a 60-degree sweep delta wing, using data from Lippisch's research and the DM-1 tests in NACA Langley's wind tunnel.

The USA already had its own proponent of the delta wing in the early 1940s. Robert T Jones at NACA recommended a thin delta for high-speed flight, and he produced detailed data on the relevant drag statistics and the optimum sweep angles for a wing with a rounded leading edge. Much debate was generated concerning the problems of devising appropriate control surfaces for a delta wing at lower speeds and means of damping its tendency to generate high roll rates in conditions of high lift.

In October 1946 Lippisch himself, after being taken to the USA as part of Operation *Paper Clip* and working at the USAAF's Air Materiel Command at Wright Field, in Ohio, was seconded to the company as a consultant on the XP-92 design. His studies persuaded Convair's chief aerodynamicist Ralph Schick that a tailless delta format would be generally preferable for the design, as Burstein had thought. At the same time, Ed Heinemann at Douglas Aircraft was working on Lippisch-inspired configurations for a project that would later emerge as the US Navy's F4D Skyray interceptor, which first flew in January 1951.

By April 1948 the XP-92 was mocked-up with a curious cylindrical fuselage that included a cockpit and four 20 mm cannon contained in a spiky nose section that was located centrally in the air intake for the ducted ramjet motor. In this respect it echoed the Miles M.52 of 1945, but with a thin delta wing and vertical stabiliser rather than the straight flying surfaces of the stillborn British supersonic jet. Fuel for the supersonic climb to interception altitude was contained in two massive underwing drop tanks. The original XP-92 interceptor, with its relatively large fuselage, was cancelled in June 1948, although research on relevant powerplants and aerodynamics continued. The

An early conceptual sketch of the Convair XP-92 point-interceptor. It reached mock-up status in 1948, with the pilot's cockpit contained in a central 'shock diffuser'. Launched from an eight-wheeled trolley, the 38-ft-long aircraft was intended to reach Mach 1.75 at 50,000 ft and intercept its prey with four 20 mm cannon, before returning to land on its own undercarriage (*Terry Panopalis Collection*)

'flying mock-up' XP-92A (Model 7-002) was sanctioned using conventional turbojet power and a high proportion of hardware from other existing aircraft.

MX-1626 was the first of a series of definitive GEBO II concepts leading to the B-58. This twin-turbojet version, drawn up on 3 February 1952, had a lower fuselage pod that was integral with the main fuselage aerodynamically and could contain nuclear or conventional bombs, radar, a reconnaissance package or 'Ferret' ECM equipment. With a three-man crew and a length of 81 ft, it relied on a B-36 'mother ship' to carry it for the first 2000 miles of its combat mission. In some versions the lower fuselage section contained a third turbojet (*Terry Panopalis Collection*)

The primary advantage of the delta compared with conventional swept or un-swept wings for supersonic flight was low transonic drag, as the delta structure enabled a thinner wing and an increase in lift at speeds up to Mach 1. At a high angle-of-attack (AoA), the lift decreased gradually without inducing unwelcome stall-spin characteristics. The long-chord wing root also allowed a lighter structure with considerable fuel capacity and great rigidity. It prevented the 'warping' effect sometimes encountered by thin, swept wings that caused 'aileron reversal' – a condition in which operating the ailerons had the opposite effect to the intended one. The elimination of the usual tailplane at the rear of the aircraft saved weight and avoided stability changes at supersonic speeds. Trailing-edge flaps were also considered unnecessary.

The creation of a large supersonic bomber was clearly more challenging, although the early configuration of the XP-92 was in effect a scaled-down version of a transonic bomber proposal for what would become the USAF's Generalized Bomber (GEBO) I requirement. Convair produced a study in 1948 that proposed a turboprop-driven aircraft with a 50,000-lb bomb-load to meet this need. The ratio of lift to drag at Mach 2 for any aircraft with a fairly conventional shape would be very unfavourable, and massive engines would be needed to sustain the speed and counteract drag. To optimise lift at high Mach a thin wing was necessary, but that implied poor low-speed handling, high landing speeds and little internal space for the heavy fuel load.

In 1945 Boeing's B-29 was the standard USAAF heavy bomber, although the company was already working on a swept-wing, jet-powered successor. Its highly innovative design, which emerged as the B-47 Stratojet proposal by the end of 1945, sought to resolve the lift/drag problems and offer high subsonic speed together with acceptable handling across the speed range and an internal nuclear war-load.

Inevitably, the B-47's thin 35-degree swept wing, using thick, heavy skins and supporting six podded jet engines, allowed little space for fuel. The B-47 therefore became a medium-range bomber, leaving Consolidated Vultee (Convair) to secure the heavy long-range bomber role with its gigantic B-36 Peacemaker until Boeing could develop the larger, more powerful, longer-ranging B-52 Stratofortress. However, the Boeing bombers were subsonic and the 'higher and faster' design impetus of that time still promised the chance of a supersonic successor to them all.

The USAAF's Air Research and Development Command (ARDC) initiated the contract process with its GEBO II in March 1949. Whereas GEBO I had generated optimistic outline concepts for bombers weighing as much as 1.2 million pounds with ranges of around 20,000 miles, the new study's aim was to explore ideas for a manned supersonic reconnaissance-bomber or 'attack system'. It attracted some highly speculative

Seen here in an immaculate white paint scheme, the XF-92A (formerly the XP-92A) was America's first delta aircraft. It was built with a conventional cockpit and nose intake for its Allison J33 turbojet and given full-span elevons for flight testing. Rows of tufts were applied above the right wing to study airflow. Fitted with a strong, 'high-speed', canopy, the XF-92A provided many pilots at Edwards AFB with their first experience of delta wing flight (*Terry Panopalis Collection*)

design studies from North American, Curtiss, Martin, Douglas and Convair, whose proposal was adopted as the most promising.

Initially, Convair sought to meet the demand for intercontinental range by using a parasite concept in which a large 'mother ship' would carry the bomber to within 1500 miles of the target and release it at high altitude and 500 mph to complete its mission, before returning to the carrier aircraft. Convair had experimented with the same principle in 1948, with a Republic F-84F or McDonnell XF-85 Goblin escort fighter being carried beneath a B-36 to protect it over hostile territory. Convair's expensive, transonic parasitic bomber featured a delta wing, four engines and a crew of two. Its radar, three engines and some fuel would have been built into a droppable pod in a section of the aircraft that returned to base.

By November 1950 Convair's designers remained wedded to the parasite concept, adding a pod that contained an expendable engine, with two more engines in underwing pods that could also be disposable. In all, five engines were considered necessary to accelerate the aircraft from its B-36 carrier, reach Mach 1.3 and travel supersonically for up to 2000 miles to its target. The return journey, with the remaining two fixed engines, would be at Mach 0.9.

A second design approach, and one that would influence the entire B-58 project, involved carrying only the bomb-load (and possibly some of the fuel) in an external, low-drag, jettisonable pod. This idea avoided the need for a large internal bomb-bay to accommodate massive 1940s-era atomic weapons, and it also reduced the need for internal fuel. A smaller, sleeker airframe would therefore be possible, using a delta wing.

Before the bomber design could proceed further the delta wing had to be properly tested on Convair's revised XP-92, with a 60-degree-sweep delta wing and a completely redesigned fuselage that included a more conventional cockpit and canopy. Re-designated the XF-92A, the aircraft was completed by 4 November 1947. Its proposed ducted-rocket engine with liquid rocket boosters was replaced by a 5200-lb thrust Allison J33-A-23 turbojet, developed by General Electric (GE) from the Rolls-Royce Derwent and borrowed from a Lockheed P-80 Shooting Star. Unlike the Lippisch designs that inspired it, the short-range, point defence XF-92A (Model 7002) had a more conventional fuselage. However, its unusually large triangular vertical tail echoed the Lippisch original.

Confounding the critics, who predicted that the delta wing would make the aircraft uncontrollable at high AoA, particularly during the landing approach, Convair's chief of experimental flight testing,

E D 'Sam' Shannon, made a successful first flight in XF-92A 46-682 on 18 September 1948 at Muroc Dry Lake, in California.

Although the USAF's interceptor requirement for the aircraft was cancelled, as was the second prototype, the XF-92A was built to prove the delta wing concept. It duly made many test flights, reaching Mach 0.95 after a more powerful (but less reliable) J33-A-9 afterburning engine was installed. USAF tests were conducted by Chuck Yeager and Frank 'Pete' Everest, the former finding the jet pleasant to fly but the latter being unhappy about its stability, noting that the XF-92A had a tendency to pitch up when turning at high speed. It could not be made to spin, however, and resisted downward pitching if the wing had stalled. Various wing fence installations were tested in 1953 to control the opposite tendency – pitching upwards in certain flight situations. Once the wing fence trials had been completed, the delta wing's inherent strength, stall-free characteristics and useful internal space were now considered proven.

Other notable test pilots to fly the first delta-winged aircraft included Fred Ascani, Albert Boyd, Jack Ridley and Kit Murray, all of whom would play major roles in the development of a new generation of USAF aircraft.

In February 1953, NACA took over the XF-92A in a new white paint scheme and test pilot Scott Crossfield made 25 more flights, taking the little delta's total to 119 before a nose-wheel collapse while taxiing ended its useful career in October of that same year. The XF-92A was even used for two 1950s Hollywood films, playing the part of a 'MiG-23' in the John Wayne motion picture *Jet Pilot* and also appearing in *Towards the Unknown*, a William Holden 'epic' about experimental test flying made at Edwards AFB, California.

DELTAS FOR THE USAF

Although the XF-92A's pioneering legacy was paralleled in European initiatives such as the Avro 707 and Vulcan, the Gloster Javelin and the Dassault Mirage, it became Convair's design trademark. Indeed, the company even considered trying to patent it. Convair's embracing of delta designs resulted in production of a series of interceptors that equipped the USAF's Air Defence Command (ADC) for decades, provided Strategic Air Command (SAC) with the world's first supersonic bomber and almost gave the US Navy a revolutionary seaplane jet fighter.

The XF-92A project led very directly to the USAF's first operational delta, the F-102 Delta Dagger, which was to serve with ADC's interceptor squadrons for more than 15 years. Twice as heavy as the XF-92A and 25 per cent larger, the first YF-102 was completed on 2 October 1953 and strongly resembled the pioneering Convair delta test bed in outline. However, twin air intakes on the fuselage sides replaced the single nose intake of the experimental jet so that an interception radar set could be carried. This comparatively innovative device had become essential for the 'collision course' interception technique that would be required to stop high-speed bombers by flying a course that predicted their path ahead, rather than merely directing the interceptor on a tail-chase route to follow its adversary.

Furthermore, Convair anticipated that the complexity of guiding a supersonic missile-launching fighter in pursuit of a high-performance bomber would also become an automated process, with the pilot as a weapons systems manager. British defence planners had already advanced a step further by abolishing the role of the pilot altogether.

Hughes Aircraft were architects and producers of the MX-1179 fire control system and its AIM-4 Falcon guided missiles that would become the heart of the F-102A weapons system. The exceptional Pratt & Whitney (PW) J57 turbojet, fundamental to the success of many 1950s US designs, became its powerplant.

Convair's chief project test pilot, Richard Johnson, made the first flight in the prototype YF-102 (52-7994) on 24 October 1953, and the subsequent test programme soon revealed major aerodynamic problems – severe buffeting and yawing – as the aircraft was pushed beyond Mach 0.9. Then on 2 November the engine flamed out on take-off with the aircraft at a high AoA, causing a crash-landing.

As part of the contract signed by Convair with the USAF, the first 40 pre-production and production F-102s were already being assembled on the assumption that the design would be acceptable for service use from the outset. Under the Cook-Craigie plan adopted by the USAF in the late 1940s, expensive, one-off prototypes were to be bypassed and most of the production tooling would be used for the early YF aircraft, with any minor modifications dictated by the test programme incorporated on the production line rather than in extensively modified additional prototypes.

Flights by the second aircraft (52-7995) established the depressing fact that the YF-102A was resolutely subsonic. By 27 January 1954 it had been dived to Mach 1.06, but with extreme instability. The wing was modified to 'Case X' configuration, with a cambered leading edge and upturned (reflexed) wingtips, and the rear fuselage was extended. Both changes reduced yaw and buffeting and Mach 1.29 was attained in a dive, although contrary to the wind tunnel-based predictions that Convair had used, the fighter still would not 'go supersonic' in level flight.

As production aircraft began to emerge from the factory in a configuration that could not achieve the required performance, Convair was very fortunate in being handed a solution to its problems by NACA Langley. In 1951 its Assistant Director, John Stack, had devised a transonic wind tunnel at the Langley Laboratory, and one of its scientists, Richard T Whitcomb, was able to study airflow patterns on aerodynamic models at supersonic speeds. He discovered that transonic drag could be greatly reduced if an airframe's cross-section was varied to form a smooth curve from nose to tail. To achieve this, the presence of a wing had to be compensated for by slimming the fuselage at the wing-fuselage joint. His 'Area Rule' was applied to the YF-102A by lengthening and completely redesigning the fuselage. The rear fuselage was bulged outwards with 'Yellow Canary' extensions, the nose was drooped and the intakes were re-fashioned to give an overall so-called 'Coke bottle' profile.

A similar process would be used for the B-58, Convair hoping that this would allow the aircraft to achieve the predicted performance figures it had promised an increasingly sceptical USAF – the latter had voiced its concerns in mid-1954 in view of the F-102's problems.

On 21 December 1954, Richard Johnson took the revised F-102 to Mach 1.2 in smooth, level flight. Intake revisions had increased the maximum level speed to Mach 1.53 by January 1956, with a taller vertical stabiliser and larger speed brakes being added in April of that year. The selection of the J57-P-23 engine established the final production configuration in April 1957, by which time about half the aircraft ordered had already left the factory. Major, very costly modifications continued until 1962 in order to bring them into line. The 'Deuce' (1-0-2, or one-zero-deuce in card-player's language) finally entered USAF service in June 1956, and its two-seat TF-102A variant would play a vital part in training B-58 pilots.

Convair test pilot Lt Col James F 'Skeets' Coleman is helped into the cockpit of the XFY-1 Pogo prior to him making a tethered take-off and landing at Naval Auxiliary Air Station Brown Field, 13 miles southeast of downtown San Diego, in August 1954. The Pogo's delta wing and large tail surfaces helped to make the VTOL prototype impressively manoeuvrable and responsive in more than 40 hours of flight testing (*US Navy*)

DELTAS FOR ALL

While F-102A development continued, Convair initiated two more delta-wing fighter design projects – one for a US Navy jet seaplane and the second to provide the same customer with its first vertical take-off and landing (VTOL) fighter. Both required very challenging technological innovation, and although they were ultimately cancelled, the aircraft yielded valuable research data on the use of deltas in previously unexplored areas of flight.

The idea behind the revolutionary VTOL XFY-1 Pogo and its rival design the Lockheed XFV-1 originated in Germany, where, by 1944, airfields were becoming vulnerable and the possibility of a point-defence fighter that required no runways was an attractive proposition. Of the two credible designs proposed by Bachem (Ba 349 *Natter*) and Focke-Wulf Fluzeugbau AG (*'Treibflügel'*), only the former was built.

The *Natter* (Viper) was a simple straight-winged manned missile powered by a Walter rocket motor with external boosters and constructed from wood. After vertically-launching from a rail-equipped 20 m-tall launch 'ignition pole platform' (a vertical pole made from a planed-down tree trunk similar in size to a street light or telegraph pole), the *Natter* would have been guided towards an incoming Allied bomber stream by an autopilot. A human pilot would have taken over the flight controls for the final stages of the interception and fired air-to-air unguided rockets at target aircraft. He would then have released the aircraft's nose section and parachuted to safety while the rocket motor section was recovered on another parachute.

After numerous unmanned tests, Lothar Sieber made the first manned *Natter* flight on 1 March 1945. The aircraft crashed soon after launch and the nose separation mechanism failed, resulting in Sieber being killed. Although the war ended before the *Natter* could enter combat, two examples were shipped to the USA after VE Day for examination.

Convair's Pogo ascended vertically, like a *Natter*, although it was hauled aloft, like Lockheed's XFV-1, by a massive 5100 shp Allison XT40-A-6 engine driving contra-rotating propellers. It then converted to level flight and landed vertically onto four small caster wheels at the tips of its delta wings and twin vertical stabilisers. It made a series of un-tethered take-offs and landings in August 1954, successfully transitioning to level flight in October. Although Convair test pilot Lt Col James F 'Skeets' Coleman became adept at looking back over his shoulder from an effectively recumbent position in order to land vertically, the difficulty of so doing for a Naval Aviator on a moving, pitching flightdeck of an aircraft carrier was a major factor in the cancellation of the Pogo and XFV-1 (which never made a vertical take-off) in 1955. However, the Pogo's delta wing and large tail surfaces had helped to make the VTOL prototype impressively manoeuvrable and responsive in more than 40 hours of flight testing.

The US Navy's other Convair project in 1952 was equally futuristic but short lived. It was effectively an F-102 derivative that would land and take off using a twin water-ski undercarriage. Encouraged by the Royal Air Force's interest in the British Saunders-Roe SR.A/1 jet-powered fighter flying-boat of the late 1940s, Convair decided to broaden its traditional interest in building flying-boats such as the PBY Catalina and R3Y Tradewind by also creating an interceptor. The company's hydrodynamic department under Ernest Stout had already sketched seaplane fighters with relatively conventional airframes in 1947, and in January 1951 the US Navy accepted a new Convair design with delta wings designated XF2Y-1. The latter's delta wing, tall triangular tail, v-shaped windscreen and pointed nose gave it a passing resemblance to a slightly smaller F-102, although the aircraft had two J46 engines with intakes above the fuselage to avoid sea-spray and a large hydro-ski that extended from the lower fuselage.

The US Navy ordered 14 development aircraft (which were to be armed with four 20 mm cannon), and the first water take-off was made on 9 April 1953 – six months prior to the first F-102 flight. Although it was never 'area ruled' like the Delta Dagger, the XF2Y-1 became the first supersonic seaplane on 3 August 1954 when it broke the sound barrier in a shallow dive. Landings and take-offs from choppy sea surfaces were demonstrated, as was recovery of the aircraft onto a ship at sea. Sadly, the first aircraft disintegrated in flight due to pitch instability during a high-speed demonstration for senior US Navy personnel on 4 November 1954.

Although tests continued with two additional aircraft until March 1957, the extreme buffeting experienced when taxiing in the open sea proved insurmountable and the programme was abandoned later that year. Although a Mach 2 version powered by a GE J79 turbojet remained on the drawing board, further useful lessons had nevertheless been absorbed by Convair in respect of stability issues with the delta wing.

The company's next delta was the F-106 Delta Dart, which was originally intended to be the definitive version of the F-102A. Using the same basic airframe as the latter fighter, but with a more powerful Wright J67 (Bristol Olympus) turbojet, MX-1179 avionics and MA-1 fire control system, the aircraft was to have been designated the F-102B. PW's J75 engine soon replaced the troubled J67, however, and in 1955 the USAF committed to 17 research and development F-102Bs alongside an F-102A order for 562 aircraft.

In this late-1952 MX-1964 mock-up, the design still has a pod, which is longer than the main fuselage and mates with it along flat surfaces, but the engines are now built into the lower surface of the wings and a 30 mm tail gun turret has been added. Another configuration placed the outer engines above the wing (*Terry Panopalis Collection*)

Re-designated the F-106A in June 1956, the USAF's so-called 'Ultimate Interceptor' was intended to reach Mach 2 and destroy incoming bombers within a 375-mile tactical radius at altitudes up to 70,000 ft – the pilot would rely on semi-automatic guidance from a network of computer-based radar ground control stations when it came to engaging the enemy. As with the F-102A, the Delta Dart carried its AIM-4 Falcon air-to-air missile armament internally. Additionally, the F-106A could also launch the bigger Douglas MB-1 Genie nuclear-capable air-to-air missile.

The Delta Dart entered service in May 1959 after a development period in which its only serious problems were associated with the Hughes MA-1 electronics, the J75 engine and the Convair ejection seat. The airframe gave further proof of the effectiveness of the delta configuration in providing manoeuvrability and low drag across the speed range. F-106A Delta Darts and two-seat F-106Bs remained in ADC and Air National Guard service until August 1988.

Paralleling its fighter projects, Convair continued development of the supersonic bomber, which, by 1953, resembled on paper an enlarged F-102 with four big engines under its wings and a massive weapons and fuel pod (inherited from its early GEBO origins) beneath its slender fuselage as an integral part of the design, rather than as an optional piece of disposable ordnance. That concept was steadily refined up to the first flight of the prototype B-58A, Convair's third production delta aircraft, on 11 November 1956 after a relatively short development period. Although it was never to use its formidable capability in action, the bomber would make a very significant contribution to maintaining America's military superiority during the Cold War.

CHAPTER TWO

MAKING IT WORK

The XB-58A, with Convair test pilot Beryl A Erickson at the controls, touches down at 150 knots at Carswell AFB to mark the end of its first flight. Although the nose-high AoA obviously restricted the pilot's forward vision, it allowed the large wing area's aerodynamic braking effect to shorten the landing run (*Author's Collection*)

Many of the ground-breaking aircraft designs of the 1950s had their development phases delayed or threatened by the slower pace of avionics and jet engine evolution compared with the dramatic advances in airframe design. GEBO II in 1950 specified a bomber or reconnaissance aircraft capable of Mach 1.5 on missions over a 3500-mile combat radius. The Soviet bloc's acquisition of operational nuclear weapons in 1949 added urgency to the project and set an in-service date of 1958 for a SAC bomber capable of delivering a load of bombs weighing between 20,000-50,000 lbs within GEBO II's performance figures.

The disposable pod idea was retained for use by the aircraft, and it was initially designed to blend conformally into the jet's lower fuselage. The pod evolved into a container for weapons, fuel and any equipment deemed unnecessary for the return journey. Initially, the GEBO II was to be powered by three GE J53 engines, one of which would be pod-mounted. This could be ejected with the pod, although it could also possibly have been used to power the pod as a guided bomb. Thousands of configurations were explored in GEBO II during 1950, and Convair calculated that its 100,000-lb parasite, pod-bearing bomber would be able to travel supersonically for 1500 miles from its B-36 carrier, deliver its missiles or bombs at high altitude and return for up to 2500 miles at high subsonic speed.

Convair's chief rival in the bomber business was Boeing, whose GEBO II designs continued in the direction that had produced the B-47 Stratojet. Swept wings with podded engines, a conventional tail unit and a tandem undercarriage all re-appeared in the Model 484. Both companies continued with design studies and wind-tunnel tests throughout 1951, Convair's research for a Long Range Bomber/Reconnaissance Airplane taking the official designation MX-1626 while Boeing's was assigned the title MX-1712 (later, MX-1965). The USAF concentrated on these two proposals, excluding any other competition. Both aimed to produce mock-ups by the end of 1952 and to fly prototypes late in 1954. The Convair proposal, re-designated MX-1964 in April 1952, received the most favourable reactions from the outset.

By the fourth concept version in March 1953, MX-1964 had an area-ruled fuselage and a completely separate pod, with its J57 engines paired in underwing 'Siamese' nacelles (*Terry Panopalis Collection*)

The design parameters for Phase I of development specified a relatively small two-stage aircraft rather than the massive GEBO I behemoth suggested by studies in the late 1940s. Its maximum radius would be 4000 miles, with a three-man crew comprising a pilot, a navigator/bombardier and a defensive systems operator (DSO) to control a 30 mm cannon remotely and manage electronic countermeasures (ECM) devices. On 5 May 1954 the defensive armament was finalised as a GE T-171 (M61A1) 20 mm rotary cannon. There was also a need for smaller nuclear warheads, as the existing W5 or W13 versions were too bulky to fit a B-58 pod.

The bomber's range was to be achieved through in-flight refuelling and its armament would include a bomb load of 10,000 lbs or an air-to-surface missile with a 50-mile range. Convair also proposed a version with a larger wing, swept at the leading edge to 65 degrees. Power would have come from twin J75 or J67 engines, or from four J57s or similar turbojets. Boeing and Convair conducted extensive wind-tunnel testing, and by October 1952 attention had turned to the selection of appropriate systems for flight and weapons control.

Although both designs appeared to meet the basic performance requirements, the USAF felt that Boeing's MX-1965 would have greater difficulty in delivering the required sustained supersonic speeds. Its development was therefore terminated in October 1952, and on 10 December, having further clarified its design in a bulky document labelled FZP-4-008, Convair became prime contractor of the MX-1964.

Two months earlier, the company's Texas factory and the adjoining Carswell AFB had been devastated by a tornado that destroyed many parked B-36s. The company was in serious need of a morale boost after working 82-hour weeks to remedy that destruction and, fortuitously, on 12 February 1953, it was told to proceed with a programme covering both the XB-58 bomber and XRB-58 reconnaissance-bomber.

This was the first time a single manufacturer had been given sole responsibility for an entire complex weapons system, Convair not only having to design and construct the aircraft, but also supply all of its spare parts and create the tools and manuals needed to service it. Although the bomber's engines were, as usual, the main items that were government-furnished equipment, Convair (Fort Worth) became responsible for manufacturing or sub-contracting virtually everything else. The company had also applied this weapons systems management concept to the F-102 Delta Dagger, as did its Astronautics Division to the massive Atlas intercontinental ballistic missile programme.

By mid-1961 almost 5000 suppliers were involved in the XB-58 project, 16 of them as major subcontractors and partners. Sperry had the vital task of creating the bombing/navigation system, Bendix took responsibility for the flight controls and Hamilton Standard's air conditioning system would keep the aircraft's sensitive components at the right temperatures at supersonic speeds, where frictional heating could cause damage.

DELTA MAJOR

Convair designers continued to define an exact configuration for the aircraft, and by April they had permission to build a full-scale mock-up with a 60-degree leading-edge sweep-back, two engines on inboard underwing pylons and two more above the wing further outboard where they would be less susceptible to shockwave interference. The same area rule principle that had saved the F-102A was later applied to the fuselage to reduce drag. It became clear to Convair that its basic design, with Mach 2 capability, might become a strategic missile carrier. Its relatively small size might even yield a strike aircraft for Tactical Air Command (TAC) or a long-range interceptor for ADC, although none of those options found USAF support.

When the MX-1964 mock-up was unveiled under conditions of great secrecy in late 1952, it had a conformal lower fuselage pod (with small canard foreplanes) that mated to the flat undersurface of the fuselage. The pod contained the aircraft's search radar, which was soon moved to the main aircraft nose, and a separate nose landing gear.

Four engines, at the USAF's insistence, were paired in 'Siamese' pods projecting forward from under each wing. Convair felt that this configuration would simplify maintenance and reduce the complexity of the installation. Also, external fuel tanks could be hung under the outer wing areas to compensate for the main under-fuselage pod, which was shorter than originally planned. The nacelles allowed for either the GE X-24A (J79-GE-1) or PW J57-P-15 engines to be fitted, but rapid development of the former engine soon made the J57 option unnecessary. However, in January 1953, it was still assumed that the first 18 aircraft out of the 30 ordered for test and development would use the J57-P-15 with JATO rocket bottles to assist take-off from shorter runways. In fact, all were J79-equipped from the outset. A 'stinger' tail gun turret and its fire control radar were included.

The production J79 engine that would power all B-58s from the outset was rated at 15,600 lbs afterburning thrust and 10,300 lbs military power in its J79-GE-5A/B version for production aircraft. The noise created by B-58As taking off with all four afterburners blazing was sufficient to cause endless annoyance to those who lived near SAC bases during the 1960s. The J79's 38-inch diameter meant low frontal drag, and it was intended to operate the engine with a variable geometry air intake to control its

The September 1953 mock-up, angled to test ground clearance at take-off, still has paired engines but the radar system is now in the nose. Drop tanks appeared temporarily under the outer wings later that month. The MA-1 rocket-propelled pod, with small wings and a canard foreplane, is visible behind the aircraft mock-up (*Author's Collection*)

maximum airflow of 165 lbs per second. The powerplant would also feature a modulated afterburner with a variable ejector nozzle. The bomber's very complex fuel system gave each engine a separate fuel control arrangement and a second supply for its afterburner. A de-icing system was installed for each engine's frontal areas.

The J79 was bench-tested in the latter part of 1953, and by 1955 it was flying in the Lockheed YF-104 Starfighter and soon to power other frontline aircraft, notably the McDonnell F-4 Phantom II and North American A-5 Vigilante, delivering up to 17,900 lbs of thrust. For the B-58, Convair worked with GE to design the engine's exhaust nozzles. The end result was a highly innovative automatic sliding cone in the centre of the intake to vary its aperture and enable air to pass into the engine at the correct speed and pressure throughout its operational range.

The delta wing's 60-degree leading edge sweepback was agreed, together with a very low thickness/chord ratio of 4.08 per cent. While the aircraft's performance was optimised for supersonic flight, its less favourable low-speed handling seemed to require high-lift additions – possibly a canard foreplane with flaps like the one used for the North American XB-70. Convair, however, chose only powerful elevons (combining elevators and ailerons) for the trailing edges.

In aerodynamic testing, which took until August 1954 to complete, the designers used their F-102 experience and gave the leading edge a 15-degree conical camber, curving it downwards increasingly towards the wingtips. They also swept the trailing edge forwards by ten degrees to comply with the area rule that gave the fuselage its 'Coke bottle' profile. At the same time the vertical tail area was enlarged.

An initial engineering mock-up inspection by senior personnel from several branches of the USAF took place in August 1953 to evaluate the modifications included in Configuration II of the design. Among the officers present was Gen Curtis E LeMay, a proponent of large, heavy bombers for SAC, of which he was the formidable commander. His cautious approach to the new technology and operational procedures required by the supersonic bomber had been forcibly expressed in 1952. After inspecting the fighter-type cockpit, his first reaction was, 'It doesn't fit my ass'. More spacious side-by-side cockpit options were modelled, but the B-58 was to retain three-in-a-row cockpits for its crew.

By January 1954 concerns about the twin 'Siamese' engine pods causing excessive heating under the wing brought about a separation of the powerplants into four Boeing-style nacelles, placed as far forward as possible with the maximum space between them. Individual nacelles also caused less drag. There were still many design decisions to be finalised in 1954, resulting in a 'stretch' of the in-service date from its original 1958 deadline to allow for further development. However, the design was essentially settled by August 1954, and a full-scale mock-up was produced with four engine pods and a separate weapons/fuel pod, although the Wright Air Development Centre (WADC) and NACA still felt that Convair's performance predictions for the aircraft were too optimistic.

Maj Gen Albert Boyd, commander of WADC and 'father' of many crucial military aircraft programmes in the 1950s, supported the B-58 against its critics and flew the aircraft himself. He emphasised the 'major advances' and the research dividend that the programme offered, but also acknowledged the inevitably high degree of risk. He accepted that the B-58 might not fulfil all of its original targets in terms of range, performance and service life – points which also seemed to be realised by SAC. Lt Gen Thomas Power, commander of ARDC and destined to succeed Le May as commander of SAC in 1957, was strongly in favour of the B-58 to replace SAC's mainstay B-47 Stratojet medium bomber, but he also felt that if SAC did not accept the B-58 it might instead go to TAC.

The B-47 was a medium-range bomber because, like most of its contemporaries, it was limited by the high fuel consumption of turbojet engines compared with piston or turboprop versions. The B-58, despite having superior engines and the benefit of large external fuel tanks in its pod, had the same basic disadvantage. However, Le May knew that the big-wing, eight-engined B-52 Stratofortress, which had made its first flight in April 1952, offered twice the B-58's range at a lower price, and it was based on proven technology derived from the B-47. It seemed to him to be a far more viable bomber for reaching targets deep inside Soviet territory.

In early 1955 it was clear that SAC's support for the B-58 was rapidly fading, citing the bomber's lack of unrefuelled intercontinental range as its main objection. At the end of 1954 Le May even went so far as to assert that it 'was not desired in the SAC inventory' and a more conventional strategic bomber would be preferable. His opposition would continue throughout the B-58's relatively brief service life. Fortunately, others in SAC valued the aircraft's high-altitude supersonic penetration capability and small size. It would be able to out-fly any enemy fighters and operate above the risk of anti-aircraft artillery. Any shortfall in its range could be compensated by in-flight refuelling once KC-135A tankers were available and by using selected forward air bases, although its unrefuelled radius was now estimated at 2300 miles, undermining its value to SAC.

Further bad news came from ARDC's figures indicating that the changes in configuration in 1954, including the revised engine positions and area ruling, still did not produce the required performance. NACA also forecast that the bomber could not fulfil its range and Mach 2 goals, prompting a late-1954 report by Convair vice-president August Esenwein that detailed the improvements that the company was making to the aircraft in order to meet these objectives.

By the end of 1954 the programme was costing $4.5m per month and it was hoped that changes in the aircraft's configuration would restore the original performance estimates. There was even consideration given to using the boron-based High Energy Fuels (HEF) that were being planned for the WS-110A (North American XB-70 Valkyrie) Mach 3 bomber. HEF, cancelled in 1959, would actually have added weight and complexity to the aircraft's propulsion systems for a marginal performance improvement.

CAUTIOUS APPROVAL

In March 1955 a B-58 Review Board was set up under Lt Gen Clarence S Irvine to analyse the whole project, and its objectives, so that it could recommend modifying or cancelling the B-58. The board's report, delivered on 10 March, proposed that the project should continue as long as its overall cost did not exceed $400m. In June the programme was reinstated with the aim of producing 13 J79-equipped development aircraft that would be used principally for exploring weapons systems appropriate for sustained, high-altitude supersonic flight. Cost-cutting was to be a major priority.

The advent of the Soviet surface-to-air missile (SAM) threat in the mid-1950s jeopardised high-altitude penetration flights, and by 1960 an SA-2 missile had downed Francis Gary Powers' Lockheed U-2 over Sverdlovsk. Ordered in 1953, the SA-2 'Guideline' missile system entered service three years later, primarily to counter CIA overflights of the Soviet Union by U-2s and SAC bombers. In October 1958 a Chinese-operated example made the weapon's first kill, shooting down a high-flying Chinese Nationalist RB-57D reconnaissance aircraft.

Although this threat had obvious consequences for all bombers, including the Mach 3 XB-70 and the B-58, an earlier report in 1953 had evaluated various bombers in the low-altitude penetration role. It included Convair's promising estimates of the B-58's performance in that role scenario, which would be very much to the aircraft's advantage when SAC was forced to shift its bombers' attack profiles to low levels in the late 1950s. SAC's view of the B-58, as its design firmed up, was undoubtedly affected by its perceived survivability problems in this new hostile environment.

However, in its revised role as a research vehicle, sufficient funding was agreed in November 1955 for the 13 Model 4 (YB-58) aircraft and 31 pods of four types offering free-fall bombs, guided weapons or reconnaissance and ECM options. These pre-production examples were initially devoid of war-fighting equipment and the M61 tail gun turret, as was the TB-58A version. In due course the complexity of the aircraft's innovative features would require all of the first 30 examples to play some part in the testing programme, although most would eventually be updated to become fully operational Hustlers.

XB-58A prototype 55-0660 is seen here around the time of its first flight on 11 November 1956, but before it had flown with a pod in place. The colour scheme was later changed to the distinctive red and white decor worn by the first batch of test aircraft. 55-0660 was a hard-working prototype throughout its test career, making 150 flights, including the first at Mach 1 and Mach 2 (*Terry Panopalis Collection*)

Construction of the first aircraft and production tooling began towards the end of 1955, by which point a small fleet of support aircraft had begun flight-testing the B-58's systems. A KC-97 was given a B-58 nose radome, radar and Doppler system to test, the radar bombing system was installed in a B-36 and the 20 mm tail gun and its Emerson XMD-7 fire control system were mounted in the tail turret of a B-47. Several F-86 Sabre, F-89 Scorpion and F-94B Starfire test-beds were used to research the B-58's stability characteristics, while numerous TF-102A Delta Daggers were allocated to provide pilots with advance experience of delta-wing flight. One major difference these aviators would encounter was the absence of flaps, which caused a nose-down pitching movement in a tailless delta. Convair's 'SACseat' ejection system, with a conventional back-pack parachute for the pilot, began static tests in February 1956.

Five months later, the first aircraft was given the serial number 55-0660 and the B-58 project was revealed to the public via unauthorised Press features as the world's first delta-winged bomber, although the Avro Vulcan had flown in 1952 and production aircraft would be delivered to the RAF from 1956.

The B-58's official name, 'Hustler', was derived from an unofficial nickname used within Convair to identify the project. Robert Widmer, who was in charge of the aerodynamics and propulsion development for the B-36 and became a chief project engineer for the company's B-58, F-111, F-16 and Tomahawk cruise missile, had picked up the suggested name in conversation with engineer Stanton Brown, and it was adopted by the USAF as a code name for the programme and eventually made official. Apart from the various pejorative connotations of the word, 'hustler' can be used to describe 'an enterprising person determined to succeed – a go-getter'. No doubt Widmer saw his revolutionary bomber in that context.

Deliveries of YJ-79-GE-1 engines began in August 1956, and 56-0660 was complete by 1 September and towed to Carswell AFB adjoining Convair's factory in Fort Worth. After extensive ground-tests of all its complex fuel, control, communications and power systems, the engines were fired up on 1 October and the sleek bomber began taxi trials exactly four weeks later, working up to a speed of 148 knots on Carswell's runway by 11 November. Convair test pilot Beryl A Erickson prepared for the first flight of the extensively instrumented prototype at 1441 hrs

A KA-56A panoramic camera was installed in the nose of the LA-1 pod attached to this 305th BW B-58A in April 1966. The camera gave horizon-to-horizon coverage, with automatic exposure control and image movement compensation based on speed and altitude data supplied by the navigator (*Terry Panopalis Collection*)

on 11 November. It lasted 40 minutes and was made with partial fuel and no external pod. Early YF-102 53-1784 was chase aircraft, flown by A S 'Doc' Witchell (who would become the second B-58 pilot), together with F-94C 51-5658.

The maiden flight was trouble-free, and all of Convair's test goals were achieved at speeds between 200-300 knots at 20,000ft over Carswell before 56-0660 touched down and its drag parachute deployed correctly. Systems specialist John D McEachern was in the second (bombardier/navigator's) cockpit and flight-test engineer Charles P Harrison in the rear (DSO's) cockpit. Erickson reported that the crew members 'were absolutely confident as we climbed into the plane'.

POSSIBLE PODS

The flexibility offered by the pod concept quickly opened up potential ways of adapting the Hustler to other roles without having to make fundamental changes to the aircraft. Convair saw that the B-58 pod could be configured in four ways with a similar external appearance. To fulfil the projected XRB-58 reconnaissance role, development of the MC-1 pod began in mid-1953, with responsibility for the camera systems allotted to the Fairchild Camera and Instrument Company – a major supplier to the USAF. As part of the weapons system contract process, other companies were drawn in to produce viewfinders, control systems and film processing facilities. The Fairchild cameras had to be reduced in size and weight to adapt to the pod's dimensions and the bombardier's cockpit panels were modified to include a photo-navigation panel in place of part of the bombing-navigation equipment.

The planned camera fit was very comprehensive and included a time recording system to print a range of data on the photographs, a camera for recording from the aircraft's search radar and a television viewfinder. Cameras for a high-altitude mission included three KA-27 36-inch 9 x 18 units similar to those included in the McDonnell RF-101 Voodoo's camera suite, three KA-25 six-inch focal length cameras in a tri-mounted horizon-to-horizon configuration and a three-inch focal length forward oblique unit. For low altitude, an alternative fit using five KA-26 three-inch cameras in a 'fan' configuration and a sixth forward oblique unit, together with a six-inch focal length KA-25 vertical camera, could be used. Only

Technicians load a single-component MB-1 pod beneath a Hustler with the aid of a purpose-built trailer with its own hydraulic raising and lowering gear. TCPs required a different version of the trailer (*Terry Panopalis Collection*)

one pod was completed but never test-flown before cancellation in 1958. A simplified LA-1 reconnaissance version was subsequently introduced in 1963.

At a time when electronic warfare was in its infancy, the USAF showed foresight in commissioning the MD-1 electronic intelligence (ELINT) gathering pod in 1952. ECM was initially used in the Korean War in April 1951 to combat gun-laying radar around Pyongyang, and the 'dark art' of anti-radar technology received some increase in funding after it was realised that new Soviet radars were being copied from American models. An MD-1 pod would have contained a wide range of devices to record and analyse electronic emissions from hostile radars. A single pod, similar in shape to the MB-1, was constructed but not tested before cancellation was executed and the hazardous ELINT mission stayed with slower aircraft such as the ERB-47H Stratojet.

There were also proposed versions of the MD-1 (known as the Ferret or El Reco) that were prioritised for jamming and ECM protection of other aircraft in a strike force. Convair also outlined a range of anti-radar and radar decoy missiles to be carried by the B-58, although carriage of a powered decoy such as the McDonnell ADM-20 Quail proposed for the B-52 would have been difficult.

The MA-1C bomb/pod version (effectively a stand-off missile) was powered by a Bell Aerospace LR81-BA-1 liquid fuel rocket motor and it contained a nuclear warhead. Small delta wings protruded at each side, three tail fins provided stability and a canard foreplane gave pitch control for guided flight of 160 miles, controlled by a Sperry-produced inertial guidance system. Its powered flight phase, lasting just over a minute, was intended to reach Mach 4 at an altitude in excess of 100,000ft. The missile then glided to its target. Twelve were ordered in July 1955, although they were cancelled in May 1957 due to the complexity and rising costs of the pod's control systems. Both Convair and the USAF also believed that the bomber could reach its target without the need for stand-off weapons.

The MA-1C was replaced in the company's design department in October 1957 by the idea of a longer-range air-launched ballistic missile (ALBM), a concept which would become a mainstay of the USAF's strategic bomber fleet as a means of extending its weapons' range. For the B-58, a relatively small missile powered by a multi-stage, solid-fuel motor would have been launched in a supersonic low-altitude 'toss' delivery and then travelled up to several hundred miles to its target.

The cheaper MB-1C free-fall pod was developed instead, and used during both the flight-test period and the B-58's early operational years. Fully loaded with fuel and a W39Y1-1 nuclear warhead, it weighed 36,087 lbs and extended for 57 ft beneath the aircraft. The pod's pylon was attached to the B-58's belly by hooks that were released pneumatically, and stability in flight came from four tail fins. Several MB-1Cs were modified as LA-1 low-altitude reconnaissance pods, with a KA-56 panoramic camera in the forward compartment and its controls in the aircraft's second cockpit.

The structure of the TCP, with its canoe-shaped indentation for the upper section to fit into the lower, is clearly visible here, as is the special trailer for this type of pod. B-58A 59-2435 *SHACKBUSTER* was used extensively for the pod drop tests, including the first drops at Mach 2 and the first delivery of a multiple weapons load (*Terry Panopalis Collection*)

A two-component pod (TCP) was also designed for a larger B-58 derivative which would fly a 'split' mission that was partly subsonic and partly supersonic. It had a larger lower fuel tank section that would be dropped first and a smaller upper warhead component, partly enclosed in a canoe-shaped trough with a rubber seal, within the upper element. As the upper component descended nose-first it released the nuclear bomb, which parachuted down to its target, allowing the bomber a short time to escape. This pod was recommended for the production B-58A in February 1958, a mock-up was completed in May 1959 and manufacturing of service items began in March 1961. Several stretched versions of the lower TCP were constructed to try and extend the aircraft's range a little more, but they were not flight-tested. All the MA-1 and MC-1 variants were cancelled on 1 May 1957, after more than $100m had been spent on their development.

The first MB-1 pod – the free-fall bomb version – arrived for testing on 31 December 1956, and it would become the standard free-fall pod. 56-0660 had made its first supersonic runs the previous day, reaching Mach 1.31 and sustaining supersonic speed for 15 minutes on the second flight. An MB-1 made its first supersonic flight in late February 1957 beneath the second B-58 (55-0661), which first took to the air on 16 February. By 29 June the aircraft had inspired enough confidence for Beryl Erickson to take 55-0660 to Mach 2.03 with an MB-1 pod attached, although the first pod drop with a dummy TX-53 nuclear warhead was not made until May 1960.

An order for a further 17 aircraft, to be designated RB-58A-10-COs and equipped with reconnaissance pods such as the MC-1 with several cameras in its forward section, was placed for fiscal year 1958 shortly before cancellation of the MC-1. They also joined the test programme and adopted the YB/RB-58 designation of the first 13 aircraft. Many were later converted to service B-58A configuration or became TB-58A trainers – the only sub-variant among Convair's range of proposals that was accepted for production.

The USAF's commitment to the programme was confirmed in March 1958 with the establishment of the 3958th Operational Evaluation and Training Squadron (OETS) at Carswell AFB to manage the B-58's introduction. Convair had already begun to train ten pilots and observers for the USAF's Category II test programme on the new bomber.

A GE technician appears to be delivering this B-58A pilot's 'missing engine' to solve his start-up problems. The 14,500-lb maximum thrust YJ79-GE-1 that powered 55-0660 and the first seven pre-production aircraft was replaced in service Hustlers by the J79-GE-5/5A that developed an additional 1000 lbs of thrust. Weighing around 3500 lbs, the engine was 17 ft long, with a diameter of 38 inches (*Terry Panopalis Collection*)

LOOKING AHEAD

Convair's interest in the 'split mission' idea grew out of the WS-110A contest that led to requests for a Mach 3 strategic bomber. In 1956 Convair felt that its B-58MI (Model Improved, or B-58B) proposal might fill that requirement, although not at Mach 3. It would have had downwards-folding wingtips, canard foreplanes, a revised 'LeMay'-type side-by-side SAC cockpit housing only two crew members in an extended fuselage and four X-207 engines based on the J79. The two outboard engines would have been jettisonable, as a rather drastic means of increasing range.

At an early stage of the WS-110 programme the idea of using massive, direct-cycle engines powered by nuclear heat to give very extended range was explored in the Aircraft Nuclear Propulsion initiative for the USAF's WS-125A requirement, and the B-58 was also seen as a potential test-bed in view of its supersonic performance. The company had planned the X-6 nuclear-powered aircraft as an early contender for the 'global reach' bomber requirement, using a converted B-36 as a reactor test-bed. The X-6 was cancelled in 1953, however, as the cost of the project mounted and its lack of feasibility became more obvious.

A turbojet-powered WS-110A bomber was more achievable in 1955, and contracts for the Mach 3 B-70 Valkyrie were issued in January 1958. Although the B-58 was no direct rival to the B-70, the Valkyrie's enormous costs and the increasing threats to high-flying bombers led to eventual cancellation of the project, which indirectly helped to increase USAF acceptance of the B-58 in 1958.

MACH 2 POWER

The timely development of the X-24A engine into the production J79 was crucial to the B-58 project, as it was the only powerplant that could meet the bomber's supersonic performance requirements. The USAF's ARDC had originally supported GE's J53 as its favoured supersonic powerplant for the three-engine GEBO II version, rather than the rocket or ramjet options offered by other manufacturers, because in 1951 it was the world's most powerful jet engine. However, GE could see that a smaller, lighter single-spool engine could be developed by using a 17-stage compressor with sets of newly-developed variable-incidence stator blades rather than the two spools used by PW. It had ten combustion chambers and a three-stage axial flow turbine section.

The No 3 engine on YB-58A 55-0671 receives maintenance at Carswell AFB on 9 December 1958. Each nacelle included two air scoops on its inner walls for cooling air that served the hydraulic oil cooler and the engine itself before being expelled through the engine exhaust. Engine changes could be performed in about three hours, assisted by the large number of removable access panels on the engine nacelles that were secured by fasteners (*Terry Panopalis Collection*)

Although the X-24A developed only 14,000 lbs of afterburning thrust compared with the heavy J53's bench-test maximum of 23,750 lbs, its light weight made the use of four engines (rather than three) in the B-58 more feasible. The X-24A also offered better fuel economy than any comparable engine.

In June 1958 the USAF's intention was to buy 77 aircraft, including the 30 test items, but the cost of the many changes and improvements that were demanded for the aircraft reduced the 47 examples for operational use to 36. Convair also officially presented its B-58B proposal to SAC, the improved design offering increased fuel capacity – both internally and in a revised pod – for increased range. It would have used uprated J79-GE-9 engines, together with a greater selection of pods including air-to-ground missiles. The USAF still had other expensive projects to support, including the B-70, and therefore showed no interest.

However, the main production order for 260 B-58As in addition to the development examples demonstrated the USAF's desire to capitalise on the $750m it had invested in the programme. Plans were laid to set up a production line at Fort Worth to build sufficient jets to equip five SAC wings with Hustlers at the rate of six aircraft per month. The first squadrons were to be operational by November 1960, allowing for production delays caused by development problems with the YJ79-GE-1 engines and the YB-58's fuel system. The latter had to be modified to ensure that the aircraft's centre-of-gravity (cg) was maintained throughout the Hustler's wide range of speeds – this was achieved by the continual pumping of fuel around its complex transfer system.

Production-standard YJ78-GE-5s were not available until September 1957 and they began flight-testing in April 1958. The J79-GE-5A (eventually modified to -5B and -5C standards) yielded 15,500 lbs of take-off thrust.

Convair's test programme plan followed a standard pattern, with Phase I becoming the manufacturer's responsibility before handing over to the USAF during Phase II. In Phase III, delayed until February 1960, SAC would refine the aircraft's combat capability and use. Before 27 November 1957, separation and dropping of a pod had not been achieved, so two development aircraft were assigned for this purpose at Holloman AFB and Kirtland AFB, both in New Mexico. Test aircraft 55-0662 made the first drop on 5 June, with the YB-58A flying at Mach 0.9 at 40,000 ft. 55-0663 followed up with the first supersonic drop on 30 September, with additional drops by 55-0672 *Lucky 13*. On 20 December the first drop at Mach 2 was made, with the YB-58A at an altitude of more than 60,000 ft.

Airframe number 4A from the initial batch, which was never allocated a serial number, became a unique static structural fatigue test item that saw it subjected to destructive forces in a static test frame. The jet's nose radome, engine pods and vertical tail were removed and it was flown to Wright-Patterson AFB, Ohio, underneath B-36F 49-2677. The latter had

YB/RB-58A 55-662, seen here at Fort Worth in 1958, lived a varied existence, initially testing pod separation, the Doppler radar and the radar altimeter in 1957. It then trialled the frangible extra undercarriage wheels and, in 1959, became the NB-58A test-bed for GE's massive 31,500-lb thrust J93-GE-3 turbojet. The jet was later converted to TB-58A trainer configuration and used as chase aircraft for the XB-70 Valkyrie's flight programme, prior to finally being assigned an operational role with the 305th BW (*Terry Panopalis Collection*)

to undertake the journey with its inboard propellers and bomb-bay doors removed and its undercarriage extended so that the incomplete B-58 would fit beneath its fuselage. The flight, in February 1957, was a reminder of the GEBO II parasite project of 1949, and of the B-58's relatively small basic airframe dimensions.

A demonstration test flight with sustained supersonic speeds between Mach 1.4 and Mach 1.56 at 43,000 ft was made in July 1957 with a take-off weight of 131,000 lbs. Further tests to establish practical mission profiles had commenced the previous month ahead of the USAF Category II tests.

After some initial hesitation, inspired to a certain extent by LeMay's opposition to the aircraft, the Hustler was now more widely seen as a suitable replacement for the B-47, offering superior performance to that obsolescent medium bomber and acting as an effective stablemate to the heavyweight B-52. In-flight refuelling trials commenced on 11 June 1958 as a matter of urgency to demonstrate that the aircraft would have adequate range to satisfy SAC's purposes. However, the USAF estimate of its unrefuelled high-altitude tactical radius of 1400 nautical miles was still significantly below the figures it had originally anticipated, and the opposition to acquiring the bomber continued within SAC HQ.

CHAPTER THREE

PREPARING THE WAY

The prototype TB-58A (55-0670) takes off for the first time at Carswell on 10 May 1960. The 1 hr 40 min flight proved the aircraft's value as a trainer, in which control could be passed to an instructor pilot in a seat that was closer to the front cockpit than the navigator's position in the B-58A (*Terry Panopalis Collection*)

The Hustler's introduction to USAF service began in January 1958 when the 6592nd Test Squadron (TS) was established at Carswell AFB to carry out the USAF's Air Force's Category II and III acceptance tests under the auspices of SAC and Air Force Systems Command. Its first aircraft, 55-0665 from the pre-production test batch, was moved across from the adjacent Fort Worth plant in mid-February, and in March the 3958th OETS was activated. It managed the flight testing and conversion of the pre-production B-58s until March 1960, when its assets were transferred to the 43rd Bombardment Wing (BW).

Early USAF crew members also worked with Convair personnel in completing the aircraft's test programmes and operational procedures. While visiting the factory, pilots like Capt Robert 'Gray' Sowers found the aircraft's sophisticated flight control system the hardest area to understand. It would indeed be the source of many of the Hustler's problems, both in testing and operational use.

One of the most pressing tasks was to prove the practicability of the various pods for the bomber. They had to be unfailingly reliable in separating from the aircraft without inflicting damage to either 'partner' and aerodynamically suited to delivery without tumbling, and the consequent risk of structural failure.

The TCP version, which became the preferred weapon in SAC use, was first dropped in October 1958 at the White Sands test range in New Mexico.

An MB-1C pod, trailing its remaining fuel, falls away cleanly from a B-58A during tests at the Holloman/White Sands range complex in New Mexico. This type of pod was chosen to begin the drop tests on 5 June 1957, which culminated in the first drop at Mach 2 from 60,000 ft on 20 December that same year. Designed to rotate slowly throughout its trajectory, the MB-1C was essentially a pair of internal fuel tanks with a thermo-nuclear warhead between them. It was the most used external stored during the Hustler's early service, although the more versatile TCP was subsequently preferred (*Terry Panopalis Collection*)

Externally, it partly resembled the MA-1 single-unit free-fall pod that was more generally used for test flights and in the B-58's service career. It had a 35 ft-long upper component (the BLU-2/B-1), with a centrally-located B53-Y1 (Mk 53) nuclear warhead, a parachute for a retarded drop and three stabilising fins. The rest of the internal space was occupied by fore and aft fuel tanks, giving a total weight of 11,900 lbs.

Below it, and partly fitting around it, with a hollowed-out trough in its uppersurface, was the lower, 54 ft-long BLU-2/B-2 section that was simply a two-compartment store for 24,100 lbs of fuel. This section, similar in shape to the upper portion but longer, was released by cartridges and a connecting rod to push it away from the upper component. After jettisoning the BLU-2/B-2 during the early part of a mission, the bomber would then proceed to the target and deliver its upper bomb-pod section, which would, in turn, eject unwanted parts of its fore and aft structure as it neared the impact point to deliver the central nuclear component.

Until May 1960 the pod tests were conducted with the MA-1 or MB-1 versions, including drops at supersonic speeds up to Mach 1.68 in April with varying degrees of accuracy. A lower section from a TCP was dropped successfully on 24 May, and on 19 November an upper section was delivered at low altitude from one of the two Hustlers assigned to these tests – 55-0663 and 59-2435. The latter B-58 made the first Mach 2 drop of an upper component on 10 February 1961, following the first supersonic drop by 55-0663 the previous December. The Hustler's weapon system was at last being proved, at least in a test environment.

REACHING THE TARGET

To avoid the new threat of Soviet SAMs, bombers had to 'go low' below the enemy early-warning and missile guidance radars. Convair's earlier predictions of the Hustler's success as a low-altitude penetrator were borne out in a test flight by B A Erickson on 18 September 1958. He completed a 1220-nautical mile course from Fort Worth at altitudes as low as 100 ft and an average speed of 610 knots, reporting a stable, comfortable ride all the way. Convair predicted that its bomber could operate effectively at even lower altitudes, although at that stage its delayed Sperry AN/ASG-42 bombing/navigation system still had to be proved operationally.

Other items of operational equipment were also slow to appear, forcing the 6592nd TS to continue its preparatory work in advance of receiving actual aircraft throughout 1960. At Fort Worth, Convair concentrated on training aircrew, producing flight simulators and other training equipment to prepare them for all aspects of the performance envelope.

By May 1959 the eight development aircraft had demonstrated the ability to penetrate US air defences on several occasions without resorting

B-58A 59-2444 heads the queue on the Fort Worth production line in a building that gave birth to a succession of Convair bombers from World War 2 onwards. This Hustler was delivered to the 43rd BW and nicknamed *Lucky Lady V*. From March 1955 all logistical support, maintenance and conversion programmes for the B-58 passed to the San Antonio Air Materiel Area, although from 1962 field teams were sent to the two B-58 bases for some maintenance tasks (*Terry Panopalis Collection*)

to internal ECM, confirming that Hustlers would be able to perform similarly against Soviet targets if necessary. The B-58's ECM capability, while never as comprehensive as that of the much larger, but more vulnerable, B-52, was also becoming very effective, and its bombing/navigation system was reaching acceptable reliability. The jet had also proved its ability to reach Mach 2, although the disturbing booms from supersonic flight over the USA were rapidly becoming unacceptable to the population generally, and compensation claims (both real and fake) against the USAF were increasing. The numbers of reportedly 'scared to death' chickens and aborting cattle were out of all proportion to the actual occurrences of high-altitude sonic booms.

Like so many military programmes of this period, the Hustler's future production was repeatedly threatened by budgetary cuts and changes. In August 1959 the production rate for Fiscal Year 1960 had to be cut from the planned 72 bombers to only 32, and then to 20, with only one aircraft per month leaving the Fort Worth line and two per month in 1961. This inevitably postponed the activation of the first operational wing, the 43rd BW, until August 1961, rather than the original early 1959 deadline, with the remaining two wings (now reduced to one) reaching readiness in mid-1963.

Delays also arose in the establishment of maintenance and training routines, the creation of handbooks and delivery of some weapons and ECM systems components. Hold-ups also originated from the unavailability of the MB-1 pod and its nuclear warhead, which were designed to allow the B-58A to perform low-altitude penetration missions, until early 1962.

Early losses of aircraft also began to reduce confidence in continued production and development. In all, 28 aircraft would be lost or terminally

Record-setting pilot Maj Fitzhugh Fulton occupies the front seat of a YB-58A, wearing the pressure suit that he used for his crew's Harmon Trophy-winning high altitude flight on 18 September 1962. The first USAF pilot to fly the Hustler, he is seen here strapped into a SACseat, as fitted to early B-58s and retained in TB-58As. Although it allowed more cockpit space, the SACseat could not protect the occupant in a supersonic ejection. It did save Convair pilot Everett Wheeler and flight engineer Michael Keller when YB-58A 55-0669, used for ECM and autopilot evaluation, suffered control failure and crashed on 27 October 1959. The second flight engineer, Harry Blosser, did not survive, however (*USAF*)

damaged during the B-58's career, most of them early on in its evaluation phase. The first crash occurred on 16 December 1958 when an electrical fault disturbed the flight controls of 58-1008 during a turn at 650 mph over Texas. USAF pilot Maj Richard D 'Smitty' Smith was unable to regain control and the aircraft entered a high-speed dive, forcing the crew to eject. Only two crew members survived, with both DSO Capt Dan Holland and navigator Lt Col George Gradel each sustaining several broken limbs and other fractures as their exposed SACseats entered the near-sonic airstream. Gradel subsequently reported that 'Everything felt wrong. Then I heard a voice which just said "Bail out"'. Smith's parachute failed to open at all.

Clearly, better protection was needed for the crew of a Mach 2 bomber, but it took another accident to release funds for a solution. On 4 June 1960, YB-58A 55-0667 was so badly damaged in a severe thunderstorm at supersonic speed near Lubbock, Texas, that Convair pilot Jack Baldridge and flight engineers Hugh Coler and Charles Jones had to eject in their SACseats. They were all immediately killed by the impact of the supersonic airflow.

By then, four more Hustlers (each of which cost $12.4m) had been lost. Two Convair maintainers died when a fuel leak in navigation/bombing system test YB-58A 58-1012 led to a fire that destroyed the aircraft at Carswell AFB on 14 May 1959. Four months later, on 16 September, tyre failure (a fairly common problem with the Hustler) forced Maj Kenneth T Lewis to try and abort a take-off at Carswell. Although he escaped, the remaining two crew members were killed in the subsequent crash of YB-58A 58-1017. Two early test examples, 55-0669 and 55-0664, were also destroyed that year, both of them probably due to loss of control and, in the case of 55-0669 (near Hattiesburg, Mississippi, on 27 October), pilot error was implicated.

The loss of 55-0664 on 7 November occurred when the aircraft and its MB-1 pod disintegrated over Lawton, Oklahoma, at Mach 2 after the Hustler yawed to the right when the right outboard engine was deliberately shut down with a specially-installed fuel cut-off switch while in full afterburner. This had been done to test airframe integrity in a worst-case scenario, with fuel transferred to the rear tanks to give an unfavourable aft cg trim situation. Similar tests had been satisfactorily conducted in previous weeks but in less demanding speed and cg conditions, and the Mach 2 test had been prepared carefully with the best available data. There was no automatic provision to close down the opposite outboard engine if this situation occurred, and the bomber immediately cart-wheeled out of control.

The vertical tail had been tested for strength in less severe yaw conditions and raised only minor concerns about its stiffness. A similar situation had occurred to 55-0666 when its No 1 afterburner shut down at Mach 1.96, although on this occasion its vertical fin had withstood loads of 45,000 lbs. However, 55-0664's red and white tail fin failed under twice that load, and sections of the fuselage began to fracture until the entire tail came away as the aircraft entered a yaw of 30 degrees to the line of flight, still at supersonic speed, and disintegrated, leaving a 75-mile long debris trail on the ground around Lawton.

Two Convair aircrew, pilot Raymond Fitzgerald and engineer Don Siedhof, were incapacitated by massive g-forces and died in the crash – their bodies were found still strapped into their seats. The second cockpit had been filled with test gear for Siedhof to monitor, and the airframe was fitted with numerous strain gauges, pressure sensors and accelerometers, whose data was sent to the test gear telemetry for transmission to Convair's engineering department ground station. Fitzgerald had been told not to use the rudder to try and correct the yaw resulting from the asymmetric configuration, and his last words before the crash were to the effect that he had his feet off the rudder pedals before operating the fuel cut-off switch.

The YB-58 fleet was restricted to Mach 1.6 for around a year following this accident while the control problems were tackled and the vertical tail structure was strengthened. A triple redundant yaw damper system was duly installed to provide automatic correction if an outboard engine failed in those circumstances. Beryl Erickson repeatedly demonstrated that the modifications had solved the problems and the aircraft was cleared for Mach 2 flight again. However, the accident played into the hands of the B-58's critics and the programme suffered significant damage in terms of reduced confidence in the design and an early end to production.

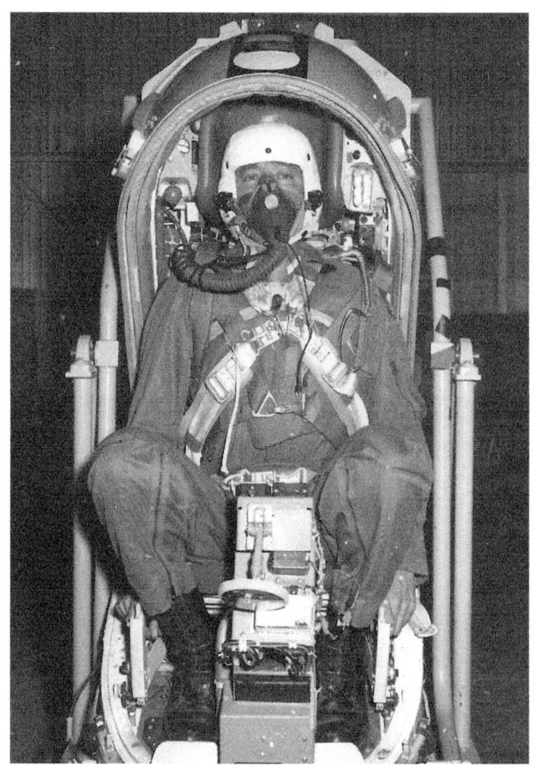

Both comfortable and confining, the Stanley Model B capsule provided the only chance of safe ejection in the upper regions of the Hustler's speed range. With a crewman in place, it can be seen why SAC imposed height limits when it selected B-58 crews. Anyone with a shoe-size above 11 could lose their toes when the capsule doors closed. This occupant's hands are resting on the ejection hand-grips which were raised before operating either or both ejection triggers. Closing the clamshell doors automatically initiated a 'Mayday' signal on the communications system (*Terry Panopalis Collection*)

By June 1960, the overall casualty list had risen to 11. The B-58 began to develop an early reputation among its opponents for inadequate safety, as well as allegedly extortionate expense. At a time when enormous funding was being requested to keep the B-70 Valkyrie project alive, the B-58 tended to be pushed back in the queue. However, as delays and problems with the extremely advanced and somewhat impractical B-70 increased, the B-58 began briefly to look more like a credible stop-gap face-saver for SAC.

These early accidents, in which several of the survivors had been seriously injured, regenerated a February 1958 project to improve the aircraft's escape systems, particularly at supersonic speeds. Conventional SACseats (also known as 'Republic' seats due to their similarity to versions installed in Republic-built F-105 fighters of that time) obviously provided inadequate protection for aircrew during ejection from an aircraft that was more than twice as fast as any of its bomber contemporaries. Its inherent dangers triggered a 'hazardous duty' pay supplement for crews. The few who attempted ejection above Mach 1 suffered severe injuries, and use of the seat at Mach 2 would inevitably have had fatal results. The $10.7m cost of devising an improved system was therefore considered essential.

Working with the Stanley Aviation Corporation, which provided many types of ejection seat for the US armed forces, Convair conceived the highly innovative Model B, which was a self-contained, pressurised, water-tight capsule. In order to squeeze into the B-58 cockpit, it had

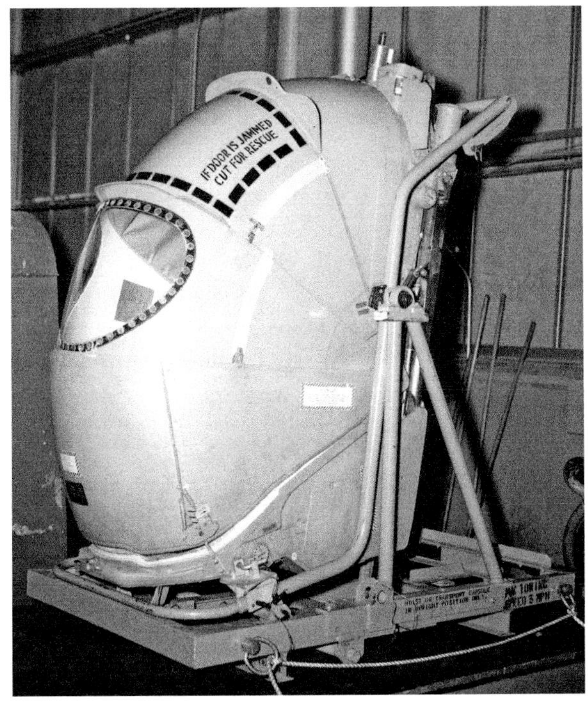

A Stanley Model B capsule with the doors closed. The pilot's version gave him a wider view of his instrument panel through a larger window, which was protected by the lower section of the doors when the capsule was open. The remaining two capsules had smaller transparencies. Each one was well-stocked with supplies of food and equipment, including an emergency radio, for a crew member to survive in virtually any conditions at sea, in desert terrain or the icy wastes of the Arctic – the latter was a reminder that most attack routes to Soviet targets would have crossed northern polar regions (*Terry Panopalis Collection*)

to fit the same ejection rails as the SACseat. The existing rails in each cockpit were slightly angled away from each other to prevent the possibility of capsules colliding on exit, although ejection was normally sequenced individually so as to avoid this happening. A collision did occur, however, during ejection from 59-2447 *RAPID RABBIT* once again near Lawton, Oklahoma, on 15 February 1962. Navigator Capt John Fuller and DSO Capt Don Avallon ejected simultaneously and their capsules struck each other, injuring Fuller, although both men landed safely.

Modified from the Model A capsule for the cancelled North American F-108 fighter, the Model B had a three-section clamshell door that was normally stowed above the crew-member's head. This instantly rotated downwards when the ejection hand-grips on the seat were raised, the occupant's knees simultaneously being forced up towards his chest into a semi-foetal position by metal retracting arms. The capsule was pressurised automatically within seven seconds of the ejection sequence commencing, making pressure suits and bail-out oxygen bottles unnecessary. The occupant was fully enclosed and automatically provided with oxygen prior to a powerful dual-unit rocket catapult ejecting the capsule from the cockpit.

The whole process was powered by compressed air drawn either from the right main landing gear strut or the capsule's own emergency air supply. In an automatic sequence, a stabilisation parachute was followed by the main 32 ft diameter parachute, typically at 15,000 ft, while the occupant remained fully protected. Landing was cushioned by a crushable section at the base of the capsule. A wide range of survival equipment was included, as well as a chaff dispenser to protect against radar detection.

If encapsulation was necessary because of sudden cockpit depressurisation, the pilot could use his controls to descend to lower altitude and the capsule could then be opened manually. The pilot's capsule included a control column (somewhat restricted in movement by the proximity of his legs) and a window that gave limited forward vision of the upper three-quarters of the instrument panel so that he could continue to steer the aircraft to a lower altitude if the cockpits suffered from sudden loss of pressurisation.

Each capsule would be separately triggered by its occupant, but the navigator and DSO had to remember to stow away their work tables. The DSO usually left the aircraft first, and an indicator lamp showed the pilot when the other crew had left. For a water landing, the capsule could float, aided by four manually-inflatable flotation bags on extended spars, while the crewman could draw air through a snorkel tube connected to his oxygen hose if there was danger of shipping water by opening the upper capsule door. In tests, one occupant was kept afloat in a capsule at sea for three days without ill effects and another (*text continues on page 44*)

COLOUR PLATES

1
XB-58-CF 55-0660, Convair plant, Fort Worth, Texas, November 1956

2
TB-58A-CF 55-0661 *MACH-IN-BOID* of the 305th BW, Bunker Hill AFB, Indiana, 1964

3
YB-58-CF 55-0662 of the 6592nd TS, Carswell AFB, March 1959

4
NB-58A-CF 55-0662 of ARDC, Edwards AFB, California, September 1959

5
YB-58-CF 55-0663 of the 6592nd TS, Kirtland AFB, New Mexico, October 1957

6
YB-58-CF 55-0665, Hughes Aircraft Company, Culver City, California, August 1959

7
TB-58A-CF 55-0670, Convair plant, Fort Worth, Texas, May 1960

8
B-58A-10-CF 58-1007 *Super Sue*, Convair plant, Fort Worth, Texas, 1959

9
TB-58A-10-CF 58-1007 *BOOMERANG* of the 43rd BW, Carswell AFB, Texas, 1962

10
YB/RB-58A-10-CF 58-1009 ***BONANZA*** **of the 6592nd TS, Edwards AFB, California, 1959**

11
B-58A-10-CF 58-1015 ***"Ginger"*** **of ARDC, Edwards AFB, California, 1960**

12
B-58A-10-CF 58-1011 ***'THE PULASKI HUSTLER'*** **of the 43rd BW, Little Rock AFB, Arkansas, September 1964**

13

B-58A-10-CF 58-1016 *CHAMPION of CHAMPIONS* of the 43rd BW, Carswell AFB, Texas, 1963

14

YB/RB-58A-10-CF 58-1018 *REDDY KILOWATT* of the 6592nd TS, Edwards AFB, 1961

15

B-58A-10-CF 59-2428 *BEN-HUR* of the 43rd BW, Carswell AFB, Texas, 1960

16
B-58A-10-CF 59-2431 of the 6592nd TS, Edwards AFB, California, 1960

17
B-58A-10-CF 59-2434 *CANNONBALL* of the 43rd BW, Carswell AFB, Texas, 1961

18
B-58A-10-CF 59-2435 *SHACKBUSTER* of the 43rd BW, Kirtland AFB, New Mexico, October 1961

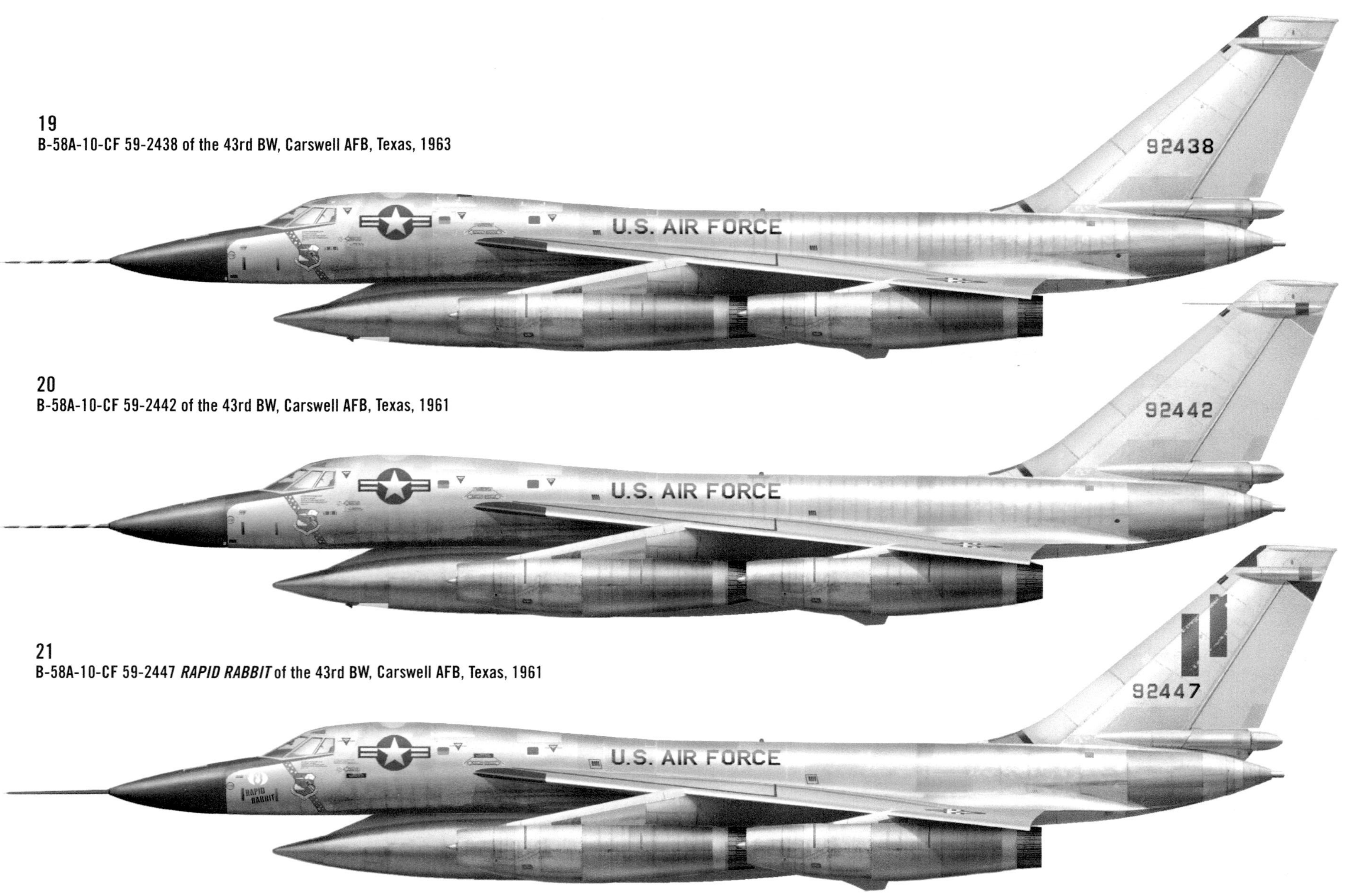

19
B-58A-10-CF 59-2438 of the 43rd BW, Carswell AFB, Texas, 1963

20
B-58A-10-CF 59-2442 of the 43rd BW, Carswell AFB, Texas, 1961

21
B-58A-10-CF 59-2447 *RAPID RABBIT* of the 43rd BW, Carswell AFB, Texas, 1961

22
B-58A-10-CF 59-2451 *The Firefly* of the 43rd BW, Le Bourget, France, June 1961

23
B-58A-20-CF 61-2053 of the 305th BW, Bunker Hill AFB, Indiana, 1967

24
B-58A-10-CF 59-2458 *STAR RAKER* of the 43rd BW, Carswell AFB, Texas, March 1962

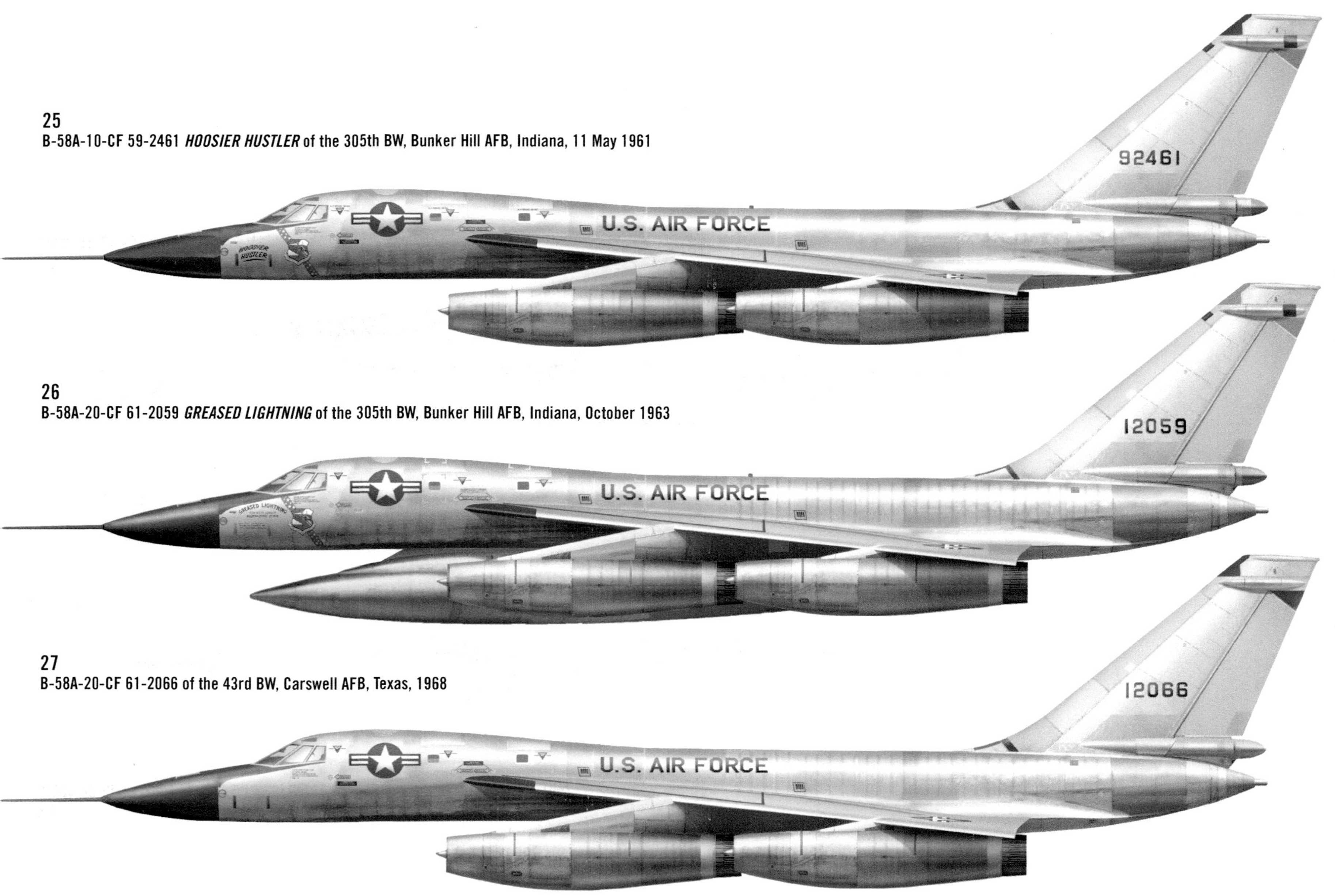

25
B-58A-10-CF 59-2461 *HOOSIER HUSTLER* of the 305th BW, Bunker Hill AFB, Indiana, 11 May 1961

26
B-58A-20-CF 61-2059 *GREASED LIGHTNING* of the 305th BW, Bunker Hill AFB, Indiana, October 1963

27
B-58A-20-CF 61-2066 of the 43rd BW, Carswell AFB, Texas, 1968

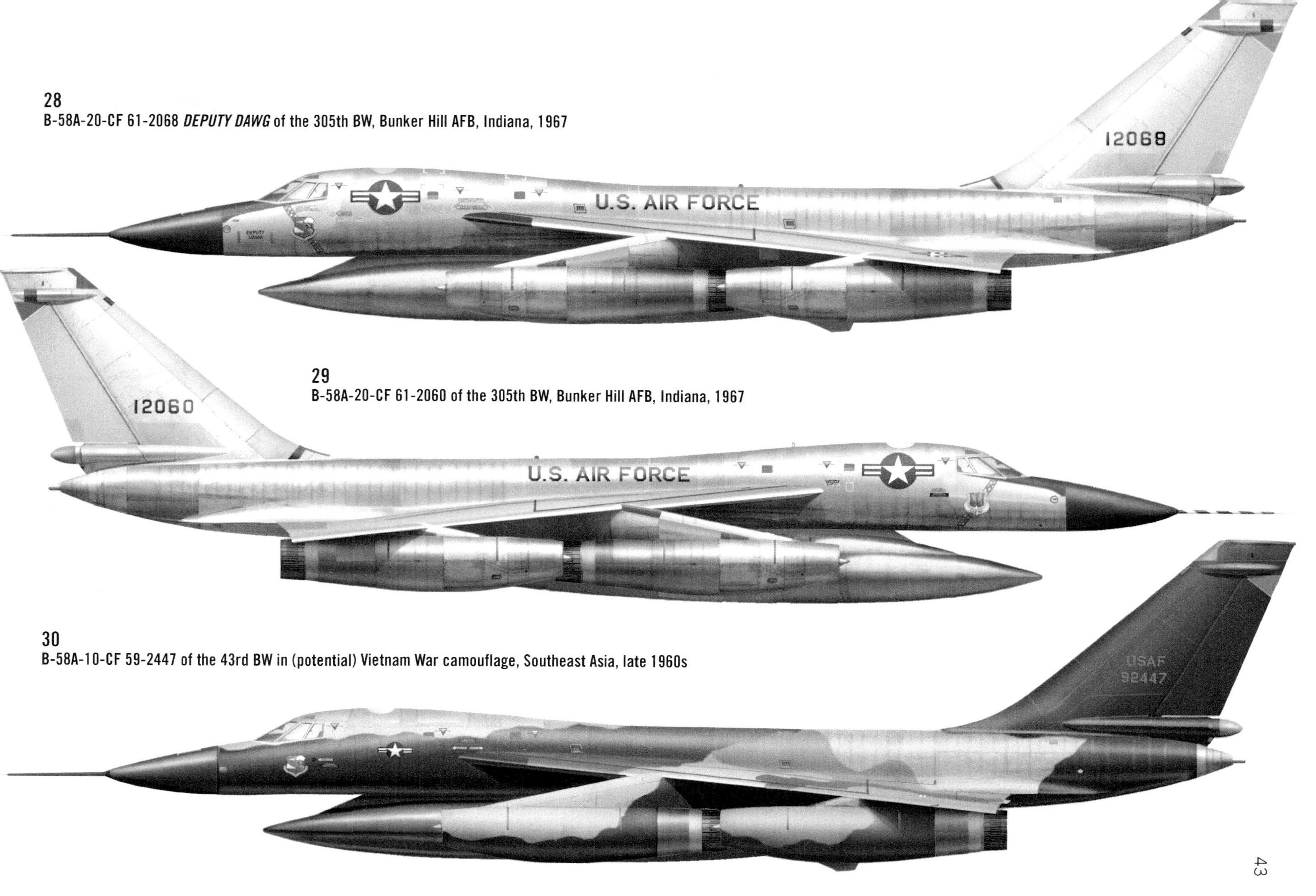

28
B-58A-20-CF 61-2068 *DEPUTY DAWG* of the 305th BW, Bunker Hill AFB, Indiana, 1967

29
B-58A-20-CF 61-2060 of the 305th BW, Bunker Hill AFB, Indiana, 1967

30
B-58A-10-CF 59-2447 of the 43rd BW in (potential) Vietnam War camouflage, Southeast Asia, late 1960s

survived an identical period on Lake Erie in the depths of winter.

The 'resident' had to lie on his back, having fully inflated the four buoyancy bags with a hand pump and then wriggled into a face-down position to retrieve the various pieces of survival gear and the radio from their stowage positions. Visibility was only possible through the small window and sea-sickness was likely.

Aircrew comfort was increased somewhat by the lack of the usual partial-pressure suits at high altitude and the restricting parachute, Mae West life jacket and exposure suit worn by most occupants of high-flying bombers. B-47 crews had to wear heavy back-pack parachutes, and early SACseat-equipped B-58 crews making high-altitude test flights donned cumbersome MC-2/3 pressure suits.

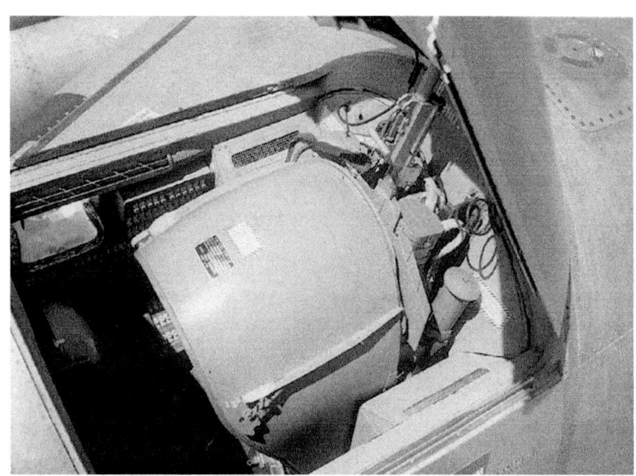

The stowed capsule doors made access to the cockpits (the DSO's in this case) a challenging athletic feat. With external vision limited by their small 4 x 6-inch side windows, the navigator and DSO were inevitably fully focused on their various panels and controls. Throughout the final stages of a SIOP mission those windows would, in any case, have been covered by thermal curtains (*Terry Panopalis Collection*)

Entry to the cockpits in any type of flight gear was made more difficult by the fitting of the stowed capsule doors poised above each seat top. When crew selection for B-58 squadrons was made, the jet's rather cramped cockpit and capsule dimensions when compared with other SAC bombers led to the elimination of crew applicants more than 5 ft 10 in tall or in excess of 185 lbs in weight.

Initial tests were conducted on model capsule versions early in 1959 and a full-scale example began a test programme on the two-mile-long Supersonic Military Air Research Track that the USAF operated on top of the flat Hurricane Mesa in Arizona in May, followed by flotation tests in January 1960. The reinforced metal capsules were attached to a rocket-powered sled and then propelled at increasing speeds along the two-mile track prior to being fired and parachuting successfully into a 2000 ft drop at the end of the track. The biggest challenge during this test period was stabilising the capsule after launch, which was done with a stabilisation frame and parachute.

Flight tests initially used a T-28 Trojan to check the capsule's basic ballistics and a B-47 for high-speed drops, followed by static ground tests installed in YB-58 55-0661 at Carswell in March 1961 and then more dynamic trials at Edwards AFB. During the latter, the aircraft was taxied at 115 mph – just above the minimum ejection speed at ground level.

At the time it was considered acceptable to use live animals for this type of test to avoid risks to humans from such untried technology. 'Yogi', a 200-lb brown bear was strapped into a capsule and successfully ground-ejected. Chimps were also used, as both types of mammal had similar organs, spinal columns and

An escape capsule is ejected from 55-0661 at Mach 1.61 and 36,500 ft in April 1962. In similar tests that month the capsule's occupant was a chimpanzee (*Terry Panopalis Collection*)

Removal or installation of a Stanley Model B capsule required a special gantry. The complex boarding platforms were also an essential part of the Hustler's ground-support package. If a landing at an unfamiliar base was required, ladders supplied by the base's fire truck department were the usual substitute. B-58A 59-2444 *Lady Luck* was a 43rd BW Hustler (*USAF*)

body mass to humans. Yogi also survived ejection from the B-58's middle cockpit at 45,000 ft and 1060 mph on 6 April 1962. The first human subject to be ejected left the aircraft at about half that speed and altitude on 28 February that same year. Stanley capsules replaced Convair SACseats in B-58As from 1962, and a version was also used in the XB-70 Valkyrie, saving a member of the two-man crew of the second example after it was mortally damaged in a mid-air collision on 8 June 1966.

B-58A 61-2062, by then assigned to the 305th BW, was used for the first installation of the definitive encapsulated seat in March 1962. Although generally very reliable, the complex system was sadly unable to save the lives of Maj Donald Close and his two crew members when control was lost of 61-2062 shortly after take-off from Bunker Hill AFB, Indiana, on 18 April 1968. However, in general, the Stanley capsule was a considerable improvement on the downward ejection system provided in the B-47 and B-52. When Convair adopted the title of General Dynamics (into which conglomeration it had been absorbed in 1953) it took the capsule idea a stage further at Fort Worth with the F-111 bomber, which had a single ejectable unit comprising the entire two-man cockpit.

FLASH-UP

Convair flew the first true production B-58A (58-1023) on 24 July 1959, followed by the second (59-2428, the 31st example to be built) which was the first to be accepted by the 6592nd TS at Carswell on 1 December 1959. Its delivery coincided with an expansion in the training of air- and groundcrew at the base. With the end of the main flight testing task in April 1959, and the B-58A's initial operating capability (IOC) planned for February 1960, the USAF explored the possibility of compensating for its much reduced order for new aircraft by reworking airframes from the first 30 test jets for operational use. Although they differed in their individual standard of equipment for test purposes, they had low airframe hours.

A programme labelled *Junior Flash-Up* was initiated in June 1958 to standardise the equipment and avionics of all but the first 17 pre-production examples. Earlier aircraft would have needed major structural modifications to enable them to operate at the tactical configuration weight of 153,000 lbs. The first five were returned to the Fort Worth plant from February 1960 for extensive modification, with another 15 being selected for similar conversion by October 1961.

The same *Flash-Up* batch of aircraft also provided the eight much-needed TB-58A trainers that SAC had anticipated throughout the development phase and eventually ordered for delivery from May 1959. Development aircraft 55-0670 was the first to be modified, the jet emerging in February 1960 and making its first flight on 10 May with Convair test pilot Val Prahl in the front seat.

The B-58A's unusual bomber configuration (single cockpit for the pilot) and unfamiliar delta-wing handling made a trainer version a vital addition to the fleet. Its extra thermoplastic side windows incorporated in the bulkheads between the cockpits (and clearly seen here on 55-0670) identified the TB-58A visually. The trainer's revised cockpit layout included offset seats to give the instructor pilot a degree of forward vision – he also had the aforementioned side windows and extra glazing in the entry hatch (*Terry Panopalis Collection*)

Another standardisation and update programme, inevitably named *Senior Flash-Up*, was begun in November 1960. This was seen by the USAF as an opportunity to improve the B-58's ECM fit and tactical air navigation system (TACAN) installation.

Boeing had modified the single-pilot B-47 with a fourth crew position for an instructor pilot or navigator and then produced 66 TB-47B crew trainers for its 3520th Combat Crew Training Wing at McConnell AFB, near the company's Wichita plant. Although B-58A production was on a far smaller scale than the 2042 examples of its B-47 Stratojet predecessor, the Hustler had a single pilot's cockpit and some challenging handling characteristics that required intensive pilot training.

TB-58As had a separate instructor pilot's position in the second cockpit, replacing the navigator's station and moved further forward. Slightly raised above the pilot's position to improve sight-lines, it retained SACseats (rather than capsules) offset to the right to provide the instructor with a very limited degree of forward vision through a Plexiglas safety panel, peering around the student pilot's seat, which in turn was offset to the left. He also had additional windows at the side and just above his eye level, rather than the tiny side transparencies of the B-58A. This was the principal external visual difference from the standard bomber variant, apart from the lack of a tail gun turret. External vision was still somewhat restricted but, as instructor DSO Dick Dirga pointed out, everyone was far too busy coping with the bomber's demands to stare out of the window from their claustrophobic 'cells'. He felt that the infamously confining back seat of an F-4 Phantom II seemed to have twice as much room as his DSO position in a Hustler.

The instructor had a set of flight controls that were linked to the front-seat pilot's. He had the same instrument panel, throttle and fuel

The addition of pylons for four B43 tactical nuclear weapons – tested on B-58A 59-2456 in 1962, seen here – added to the aircraft's number of potential targets per mission, and thereby considerably increased SAC's overall deterrent force. The one-ton weapons needed a purpose-built addition to the standard MB-1 bomb-loading vehicle to raise them into position for mounting to the underside of the Hustler (*Terry Panopalis Collection*)

controls, together with a duplicate electronic control panel. Mission electronic systems were deleted. Fuel capacity was reduced as training flights would rarely exceed three hours' duration. The consequent reduction in maximum taxi weight by 17,000 lbs made for a more sporty take-off performance, with an average time between brake release and rotation (at 160 knots) of under 20 seconds – more than ten seconds less than a loaded B-58A. Differences in maximum take-off weights were even greater, typically 160,000 lbs for a B-58A against 120,000 lbs in the case of a TB-58A.

The third TB-58A cockpit had no defensive electronic systems equipment. Another student pilot could, however, sit in it for flight experience and exchange places with the flight instructor in order to take the controls if required, potentially squeezing through a very narrow 'passage' between the cockpits that was normally used simply to pass food and drink forward to the pilot in the B-58A. A cord line was set up between the cockpits and a plastic pouch could be slid along it containing messages or decoded authorisation 'Go Code' information about a nuclear attack, which had to be compared with an original version and approved by all three crew before the bomber could attack a real target. Trainer versions had no bombing/navigation equipment or autopilot.

The first TB-58A was delivered to Carswell on 13 August 1960, and all eight survived into retirement despite intensive utilisation. 55-0663 suffered severe fire damage to its cockpit when an oxygen leak ignited while the jet was being serviced between flights at Grissom (formerly Bunker Hill) AFB in January 1969. Since the Hustler was by then on the cusp of retirement, it was only cosmetically repaired and subsequently used as a gate guard at the airfield.

A B-58's suspended pod weapons and fuel system enabled it to become a credible supersonic bomber, but it clearly limited its strike capability to a 'single-shot' bomb or missile option. By the early 1960s, strategic planners were beginning to look for greater flexibility and exploring the option of carrying conventional weapons for limited, non-nuclear conflicts and peacekeeping operations, as well as the smaller, tactical thermonuclear stores such as the B43 or B61.

Tactical strike fighters like the F-105B, F-101A, F-100D and F-84F that had been standing on nuclear alert with a single tactical nuclear weapon were being adapted to carry standard high-explosive ordnance. SAC's B-52s were also about to be given this expanded capability, although the bombers' nuclear deterrent role remained the principal priority. The ability to strike several targets with tactical nuclear weapons in one mission was considered a worthwhile modification programme for the Hustler.

The complex landing gear retraction is in progress on this TCP-carrying operational B-58A, with the nose gear about to fold back on itself before stowage. Nose-high take-offs are a delta-wing characteristic, and the B-58's long, stalky undercarriage prevented the tail from scraping the runway. A pilot's first few landing attempts often included a series of bounces that were instinctively counteracted with 'forward stick'. This merely increased lift and then induced a rapid sink rate when the control column was returned to neutral – a phenomenon known as 'elevon coupling' (*USAF*)

In January 1962 B-58A 58-2435 began test flights of a multiple weapons system that involved fixing stores pylons under the wing-root area on both sides. In addition to a pod, up to four Class D B43s, each weighing 2100 lbs and rated at up to one megaton yield but classified as 'small weapons' compared with the pod, could be carried on the pylons. Although the pylons had a very small effect on aerodynamic efficiency, the bombs inevitably added drag. They could be dropped with retarding parachutes and detonated by an impact spike that was usually covered by a jettisonable nosecone.

After initial tests of the pylon installation in February 1961, conversion kits for all B-58As from the 87th airframe onwards were ordered. After successful flight tests, including drops of the 12 ft-long weapon at speeds up to Mach 2, the modification was cleared for operational use in March 1962. With it, each B-58A could carry nuclear bombs totalling 13.4 megatons. SAC's Single Integrated Operational Plan (SIOP) required 32 B-58As to be available, carrying a total of 160 weapons and forming a significant part of the requisite SIOP total of 932 operational bombs.

Aircraft standing on nuclear alert had live weapons on board, which required intensive security but also created problems for the maintainers, as flight control systems technician Neil Byrd recalled;

'One weekend I was part of a team that had to replace the power control linkage assembly [PCLA] on a bird in an alert hangar. The plane was armed. The PCLA was located toward the rear of the aircraft near the elevons, and within feet of the external nuclear weapons. It required a specially-designed winch and cable mechanism for lowering and raising the assembly into the aircraft. We worked under the watchful eye of a serious-looking Military Policeman with an M16 rifle.'

PRODUCTION STANDARD

The Hustler's 'small but tall' appearance, with a slender fuselage and stalky undercarriage giving it a height of 31 ft 5 in for a wingspan of 56 ft 10 in, was the inevitable consequence of moving the aircraft's weapon load and much of its fuel to a massive external pod. Although the slender fuselage left little room for internal equipment, it had to accommodate three crew members – half the crew complement of a B-52.

The four engines and their long afterburners required large nacelles remote from the wing on pylons to dissipate heat and provide the most

A B-58A's immensely strong main landing gear, with its long drag strut (foreground) to extend or retract it. The twin-tyre units of the main undercarriage were small and light enough to be changed by one man in around 15 minutes (*Terry Panopalis Collection*)

favourable aerodynamics. Their relatively small frontal area helped to make the aircraft's overall radar signature far less than that of SAC's heavy bombers, according to statistics established by the Rand Corporation.

Convair designers were able to meet the required demands for airframe weight and structural strength by using honeycomb sandwich panels fixed to spars and a small number of bulkheads for substantial parts of the structure, including 90 per cent of the wing panels. There were shallow bulges above the inboard wing area to accommodate the massive main undercarriage units. Although the main wheels were only 22 inches in diameter, the wheel-well boxes in the thin wing needed a little more depth for the two four-wheel trucks. The wings' leading edges were brazed sandwich structures, able to withstand supersonic temperatures of 260°F. The wing was built integrally with the fuselage, which meant wing replacement as a means of prolonging fatigue life was impossible.

An innovation at the time, honeycomb used a core of metal or fibreglass cloth and resin with alloy skins bonded with adhesives. Stainless steel skins were necessary for components that required greater load-bearing strength or heat resistance, and the honeycomb panels provided insulation for the fuel tanks that occupied most of the wings' interior space. Overall weight-saving was considerable, and structural tests on airframe number 4A showed that the honeycomb structure was far stronger than had been anticipated. Above all, it gave a very favourable 13.8 per cent ratio of basic structural weight to maximum take-off weight. Honeycomb was also considered to be capable of surviving the aerodynamic heating (up to 325°F) and stresses of flight at sustained speeds of up to Mach 2.4, as well as manoeuvring flight with loads of up to 3g at the Hustler's operational combat weight.

As an additional bonus, the smooth external surfaces made possible by bonded panels reduced the B-58's radar signature. Airbrakes were considered unnecessary, resulting in additional weight saving, although cutting the throttles at supersonic speed brought very rapid deceleration.

More conventional semi-monocoque construction using longerons and bulkheads covered by aluminium skins was employed for the fuselage, with honeycomb panels covering the vertical fin's internal structure of ribs and spars. Aluminium alloy skins were used for the rudder, however. The fin, with a leading edge swept at 52 degrees, covered an area of 160 ft^2 (this figure included the rudder).

Pitch and roll control were provided by two very powerful steel sandwich elevons that took up an eighth of the total wing area of 2996.05ft^2. Operated by ten actuators, without the benefit of fly-by-wire electronics, the elevons could be deflected manually ten degrees downwards or 23 degrees upwards for take-off.

Most of the time all flying control surfaces were linked to an automatic flight control system, with an automatic trim system and three-axis damping. An electro-mechanical ratio-changer varied the sensitivity of the control column for the elevator function of the elevons to prevent excessive g-loads on the airframe and improve overall flying qualities throughout the speed range. The pilot could choose automatic ratio-changing or manual settings for take-off or landing. An aileron-rudder interconnection controlled a tendency to yaw when aileron movements were applied. All the flight control systems relied entirely upon hydraulics driven by the engines, so multiple engine failure immediately made the aircraft completely uncontrollable.

The fully steerable nose landing gear was a similarly complex structure that needed a hinge at its mid-point so it could fold back into its well without striking the nose of an underfuselage pod. The tyres on this and the main landing gear were inflated to 265 psi and lasted for about ten landings, and they were one of the aircraft's most common sources of trouble due to the heavy wear and stresses forced upon their small dimensions. Landing gear had to be extended or retracted below 304 knots (*Terry Panopalis Collection*)

As Neil Byrd explained, 'The delta wing of the Hustler required the pitch and roll controls to be combined into movement of two elevons. The unit that performed this function used mechanical mixing by a complex assembly – four feet square and a foot high, it consisted of rods, wheels and servo actuators that seemed to me to resemble two bicycles run through a trash compactor. Two concentric pulleys with cables running from the pilot's station were its mechanical inputs. It was called the PCLA and it was our responsibility. It contained the AFCS [Automatic Flight Control System] servos whose motion would combine with pilot stick inputs.

'Knowing that this complex, precision, highly important assembly directly controlled the elevons was sobering. We lost a B-58 one day and I will never forget the sombre mood in the shop. Whether or not the PCLA had anything to do with the crash, we all knew that it was suspected. I worked with a talented group of young men and we all knew that anything to do with flight controls was a serious matter.'

One of the Hustler's most distinctive features was its intricate landing gear, made by Menasco and the Cleveland Pneumatic Tool Company. Its high-strength steel components had to be long, strong and heavy to allow carriage of a weapons/fuel pod at an all-up weight approaching 160,000 lbs. On take-off the aircraft had to be able to rotate to a 17-degree angle of incidence without its tail scraping the runway. The steerable, twin-wheel, double-jointed nose gear leg hinged forwards at its mid-point on retraction so that the wheels cleared the nose of an under-fuselage pod.

Extending and retracting the two main gear members was also a complicated process in which the whole structure had to be compressed via double gatefold joints to lie flat in the wheel-well within ten seconds of take-off. The four wheels on each truck had two tyres apiece, separated on production aircraft by an extra wheel hub that was designed to take the strain in the event of tyre failure. It could be eroded away by contact with the ground without damage to the multidisc braking systems on each wheel or the undercarriage assembly itself. Tyres were inflated to 265 psi with nitrogen. While there were occasional breakages in the landing

Some highly skilled flying by a pilot from the 6592nd TS enabled 58-1018 *REDDY KILOWATT* to survive an emergency landing at Edwards AFB after the left main landing gear had partially failed on take-off on 19 September 1961 (*USAF*)

gear components and tyre failures were not uncommon, the elaborate engineering involved in their design produced generally reliable results.

Maximum take-off speed was not supposed to exceed 250 mph on a ground-run of 7850 ft, with rotation at around 6000 ft. If the gear was not down and locked correctly, the pilot was alerted by a buzzer and an emergency nitrogen-operated extension system could be used, triggered by the emergency brake and landing gear handle on the pilot's lower left console. A 28-ft diameter braking parachute, stowed below the rear fuselage ahead of the tail gun compartment, considerably reduced the landing run to about 2580 ft at 63,000 lbs landing weight. It could be deployed at speeds of up to 218 knots, and it was possible to complete a landing run successfully without having to use the parachute.

One advantage of so many landing gear wheels was seen when a 43rd BW jet took off trailing fire from a fuel leak that had ignited in the afterburner heat. The left main undercarriage would not retract and a T-33 chase aeroplane was sent up to inspect it. The landing gear seemed to be damaged and darkness meant that the bomber had to stay airborne and head for Edwards AFB until daylight allowed for a proper inspection to be performed. It could then be seen that the left main gear unit had jammed at a 45-degree angle and three wheels were missing. After having taken more than a million pounds of fuel from a tanker during the night, the crew dropped their pod over the Edwards range and landed safely on a foamed runway after 14 hours in the air.

Designing the fuel system was a major undertaking because up to 100,000 lbs of fuel in the pod and two huge internal tanks – one occupying much of the forward fuselage and wing and the other in the rear part of the fuselage and wing – had to be controlled in order to preserve the cg at a wide range of speeds. As the latter increased, the aircraft's centre of lift (or lift vector) moved progressively aft, requiring re-balancing of the aircraft through the shifting of fuel. During cruise, flight fuel was drawn from both forward and aft tanks to maintain balance, but with afterburners lit the fuel came only from the aft tank to maintain the required rate of flow to the engines. The preservation of cg by adjusting the elevons slightly upwards was one of the DSO's tasks.

Mounted in its flexible tail housing, a GE T-171E3 (M61A1) rotary 20 mm cannon projects below its Emerson MD-7 fire-control radar in 43rd BW Hustler 58-1018. The solid state analogue fire-control computer installed in the B-58 was the first of its kind. The small, dark square area below the fuselage was the ejection door for spent shells. To its right are the doors for the braking parachute (*NARA*)

Also, fuel could flow between openings in the wing structure, with valves preventing it from sloshing in one direction under conditions of rapid acceleration. A reservoir tank near the cg and a balance tank in the rear fuselage helped to keep fuel distribution even. On the ground, it was pumped in through a single-point coupling in the nose-wheel well or through three fillers above the fuselage by gravity. A 'wing heaviness' control and valve system corrected any tendency for fuel to be moved into one wing more than the other at high Mach due to the Coriolis effect in the northern hemisphere that impels the fuel away from the equator and causes 'fuel stacking' in one wing. This phenomenon was a suspected cause in the crash of YB-58A 55-0664 on 7 November 1957.

Production aircraft were powered to Mach 2 by four J79-GE-5A (later modified to -5B standard) turbojets, each generating 15,600 lbs of afterburning thrust for take-off and proving to be well suited to the B-58A. Total fuel consumption at Mach 2 was 1000 lbs per minute. The -5C version, offering another 930 lbs of dry thrust, was initially specified for frontline Hustlers, although the -5B version remained in use beyond 1966.

The close-fitting engine nacelles were tested in NACA's supersonic wind tunnel early in the programme to ensure that cooling air could flow smoothly around the J79s. Air was guided from the sharply-contoured circular leading edge of each nacelle, its volume being controlled by a spiked cone that moved fore and aft on a telescopic slide – the latter was controlled automatically by a hydraulic ram. For take-off, the cone was retracted into the intake to allow the maximum volume of air to pass through, and it gradually moved forwards as speed increased. Automatically activated, it began to travel forwards at Mach 1.42. By Mach 2, the cone had extended fully to keep a shock wave ahead of the intake, rather than entering it and causing a stall. It thereby controlled air passing through the inlet guide vanes and into the engine at the correct pressure.

Combined with convergent-divergent afterburner nozzles at the other end of the engine nacelle, this was one of the earliest examples of this type of supersonic intake and nozzle combination, and also one of the

The pilot's front panels, which varied slightly during production. His view through the window of the Stanley Model B capsule when it was closed covered all this area above the top of the control column. Standard flight instruments are on the left side of the main panel and four sets of engine dials occupy the right side, indicating pressure ratios (top), tachometer readings, exhaust temperatures, fuel flow, nozzle position and (lowest) vertical velocity. The Machmeter is the topmost of the larger dials, with the altimeter immediately below it and the airspeed indicator to the right of that. The second cockpit in the TB-58A had a similar front panel (*Terry Panopalis Collection*)

most successful from the outset. By effectively covering the engine compressor blades at high-speed, the cone also reduced the aircraft's head-on radar signature.

TAIL STING

Despite the B-58A's high speed and advanced ECM fit, it was considered necessary to provide the jet with defensive armament like other SAC bombers in case enemy fighter pilots chose to attempt an interception from the rear – the only direction from which they were likely to be able to approach. A twin-barrel T-182 gun was the first choice, but then the GE T-171E3 (M61A1) rotary cannon became available.

The weapon fired its 1120 rounds in two-second bursts (with a minimum of ten seconds between bursts) totalling 12 seconds at the rate of 4000 rounds per minute. Ammunition was drawn along a hydraulically boosted flexible chute from two boxes located just ahead of the gun. The latter was fitted on a gimbal mounting made from flexible tapered rings that allowed the gunner to shoot within a 60-degree cone-shaped field of fire. Cartridge cases and links were ejected from a hatch below the gun, and the whole ammunition load could be jettisoned in an emergency at the press of a button by the DSO.

An Emerson Electric MD-7 fire-control system (which introduced solid-state analogue computing to this type of installation) searched for the target, tracking it either automatically or manually within a range from 750 ft to 22,000 ft. The DSO aimed the gun using the radar, whose antenna was located above the gun turret, and a small joystick controller to his left. Viewing the target remotely on his B-scope radar display, the DSO could fire the gun by pressing the red firing button at the lower right corner of his fire control panel.

Although the system had to warm up and stabilise its gyros prior to use, former DSO Howard Bialas recalled that, 'It worked well, and I never experienced a time delay on the MD-7. I do recall spending part of an evening watching those heroic gents loading live ammunition in less than ideal weather conditions. It was cold, windy and dark, but they got the job done and I fired the whole load the next day. You had to install an external hinge to swing the gun turret so that you could load the bullets into the ammunition cans while standing on a swaying maintenance stand about six to eight feet above the ground'. Twice a year DSOs had to fire off 4000 rounds for practice over a gunnery range.

Basic flights were possible with only two crew members, with a DSO being essential for all tactical operations as some of his functions equated to those performed by the co-pilot in the B-52 or the B-70 Valkyrie – notably management of the complex fuel system. For this vital task he had a fuel monitoring panel and repeater gauges telling him airspeed, altitude, the aircraft's cg and the positions of the elevons to ensure that the airframe was not over-stressed.

With the pilot's seat slightly off-set to the left of the centreline, an unusual curved display arrangement was possible for the side panels. They included (from the left) the fuel control panel, the air conditioning controls, electrical controls, warning and caution lights and the bomb panel. The long, horizontal panel contained hydraulic pressure indicators and oxygen and lighting controls. At the base of the console was a rectangular storage space for the all-important map and data case that the pilot would bring on board for each mission (*Author's Collection*)

As instructor DSO Dick Dirga pointed out, most SAC multi-engined aircraft had two pilots, and the sophisticated systems in the B-58 made the DSO's task as substitute co-pilot unusually demanding. His rear cockpit also contained controls for ten AN/ALE-16 chaff dispensers that were installed in the main gear fairings above the wings and ejected through slots, as well as the AN/ALR-12 radar warning receiver. His responsibilities also included management of the AN/APX-47 identification, friend or foe equipment and the innovative AN/ALQ-16 radar track breaker – a Sylvania-manufactured system that was finding its first military application in the B-58, the AN/ALQ-16 acting as a major source of protection for the bomber. There were also hundreds of circuit breakers on each side panel of the DSO's cockpit, and he had to be able to identify and replace a failed one, often by touch.

Former DSO and Bendix Trophy (a transcontinental, point-to-point race held in the USA from 1931) winner Capt John Walton summed up his busy life as part of a B-58 crew;

'The DSO was responsible for flight engineering, ECM, radio communications and gunnery. On the Bendix flight my primary job was to carefully monitor the cg and make adjustments to gain the maximum performance for the speed run.'

All three cockpits had two compartments for storage of standard USAF cold sandwich snack packs, and they were also furnished with two pint-sized vacuum flask stowage holders, ashtrays and a vital two-pint 'relief flask'. Pilots who had flown the B-52H version of the Stratofortress, with its more advanced instrumentation and television displays, considered the B-58 cockpit rather old-fashioned by comparison.

At the heart of the systems required to guide a B-58 to its target was the Sperry Gyroscope Corporation AN/ASQ-42 bombardment and navigation system, an agglomeration of 18 units including the high-frequency Raytheon AN/APN-113 Doppler radar in the nose and six antennas and receivers in the rear of the aircraft, all of which weighed more than 1700 lbs. Of this, 1200 lbs was taken up by the system's massive analogue computer, operating with numerous vacuum tubes and mechanical devices. The Doppler radar constantly supplied the navigation computer with accurate ground-speed readings while the computer compensated for wind-drift as it managed heading and speed.

The navigator/bombardier's station contained the most panels and controls. On its right side was a small auxiliary flight control panel (black dials), together with the radar control handle (bottom) with which the navigator could direct both the aircraft and navigation controls (left) (*Author's collection*)

A crucial element in the equipment was the inertial measurement unit (IMU) or 'stable table', one of the earliest inertial systems fitted into a military aircraft. Complex and highly innovative, with a gimballed platform, gyros and accelerometers, it was a major source of the development delays in the Hustler's early years. Nevertheless, the IMU became an extremely accurate means of long-range navigation. It included a punched paper printer that issued data on time, altitude, position and speed to replace manually-kept flight records. Post-mission, an evaluator then had access to that data from the whole flight. Also, a camera recorded the images from the navigator's radar screen for later analysis.

Navigation aids by Bendix and Motorola were included, with a KS-39 telescopic astro-tracker (a valuable innovation that became standard equipment in most SAC aircraft) and AN/APN-110 radio altimeter for flight below 5000 ft. Although the latter was very accurate above 750 ft, it was easily confused if the aircraft was flying above thick ice or snow, which absorbed radio and radar waves. The pilot or navigator could set pointer markings on their instruments for set altitudes, and a warning light would illuminate if the altimeter detected that the aircraft had descended below their settings.

Although some of the 'black boxes' were standard items, many had to be re-shaped and tailored to fit inside the confined spaces within the airframe. Bendix Aviation Corporation's Eclipse Pioneer Division provided a sophisticated autopilot (one of the most advanced to be installed in an aircraft at that time) capable of keeping the aircraft at a set Mach number and altitude automatically or allowing it to follow a pre-set course. The autopilot also coped with all-weather landing approaches, allowing the pilot to use his manual controls without having to disengage the autopilot function.

When fully developed the navigation/bombing system's functions, many of them automatic, could provide ballistics computation, 'great circle' steering and astro-tracking, automatic radar photography and storage of route waypoints and offsets. Many parts of the system were still heavily reliant upon vacuum tubes and mechanical analogue devices, with consequent over-heating that could fill the cockpits with smoke and fumes – one reason why crews flew most missions on 100 per cent oxygen. Electronics were susceptible to heat damage in their pre-digital form, although some early digital replacements were available towards the end of the aircraft's career.

Controls for the navigation/bombing systems were arranged in the second cockpit, including a panel directly in front of the navigator for storing and displaying offsets to be used in the flight and bombing run. Below it was the indicator panel and circular screen for the search radar, which could operate in automatic or manual modes. Its cross-hairs could

The complete B-58A. AFSC's 59-2456, used for multi-weapon tests and a record altitude flight prior to being transferred to the 43rd BW, was photographed with both parts of a TCP, four B43 shapes and a 'spare' tail section, including the gun and its fire control system. The crew are standing next to the weapon's 20 mm ammunition (apparently all 1200 rounds) in the orange flightsuits that were standard aircrew apparel until the Vietnam War made their conspicuous appearance too risky (*USAF*)

be placed on a known fix-point and the radar switched to standby so that it did not emit radiation to give away the aircraft's position to ground stations. When the navigator saw on his mileage indicator that the B-58 was approaching the point marked by the cross-hairs, he could turn on the radar to check that it was still focused on the correct target and then, if he wished, switch off again until the target was closer. Navigators coming from B-47 squadrons found that the B-58's navigation/bombing systems were far superior to the equipment installed in the Stratojet.

Many of the relevant AN/ASQ-42 components were flight-tested in specially constructed nose radomes attached to B-36B 44-92052 and KC-97F 51-332. The Hustler's innovative weapons delivery method required a system that would calculate an accurate flightpath for a pod-mounted bomb or air-to-surface missile dropped from high altitude and travelling long distances to a target. A Kollsman KS-39 astro-tracker assisted in providing an accurate heading, working with other navigation elements or TACAN to compute distance to the target without visual ground references or frequent search radar transmissions far more precisely than previous systems. The astro-tracker could track stars in daylight conditions, and it was used throughout missions to provide constant course adjustment by using a selection of stars onto which it had locked at the start of the flight.

The cockpit instrumentation also included an early version of the Voice Warning System (VWS) known to pilots as 'the bitch', which transmitted warnings of any emergencies, fires or systems failures with a soothing but insistent, recorded, female voice. VWS announcements were preceded by warning lights. Close monitoring of all these systems by the crew was vital, particularly fuel management to ensure that cg and g-forces remained within limits to prevent over-stressing of the airframe. Fuel management required the DSO to enter the selected cg position, after which the fuel would be automatically moved around the aircraft's tanks to maintain that position throughout the speed range as it burned down. The B-58's inflight safety relied on accurate fuel management, and this was one of the key reasons why the Hustler had to be flown by SAC's most highly qualified and experienced crews.

MAIN LINE

The idea of giving the B-58 reconnaissance capability was revived in 1963 with Project *Main Line*. Ten MB-1C pods were given a single forward-facing KA-56A panoramic camera in their forward munitions equipment bay and designated LA-331A (or LA-1) for low-altitude photography, using up to 1000 ft of film from a removable magazine. At 500 ft and Mach 1 the camera could resolve small details very effectively, and training routes were established to develop the necessary skills required for photo-reconnaissance. Mission success rested on the combined efforts of all three crew members, who had to establish check-points on the map and maintain correct speed, altitude and heading during the photo runs.

Forty-five B-58As received the requisite LA-1 modifications to their weapons systems and cockpits, and the 43rd BW selected former RB-47 pilot Maj William S Boughton (who had previously flown low-level reconnaissance missions in the Stratojet) to manage a unit within the wing charged with conducting photo-reconnaissance operations – the latter got underway in January 1964. Prior to reaching a photo-target, the LA-1 required five minutes to warm up. The navigator, who was responsible for selecting manual or automatic operation, controlled the system via a panel that was fitted in the second cockpit in place of the weapon release equipment.

The 43rd BW tested the system over Matagorda Island, off the coast of Texas, in March 1964, followed by a supersonic run over a small objective in Vinto, Louisiana. First-class photographic results were achieved on both occasions. Later that month the 43rd BW photographed the effects of an earthquake in Alaska for the US government, with two aircraft making flights over the area at an altitude of 5571 ft despite terrible weather, a low cloud-base and dangerous terrain. Several more flights were made on 28 March by other Hustlers at a lower altitude, with U-2s and RB-47s covering the area from higher ceilings. Twelve crew members received Air Medals for their efforts over Alaska.

For a time, Carswell kept two LA-331-equipped aircraft ready for use in photographing natural disasters. Two Carswell B-58s deployed to Zaragoza, Spain, for a very successful operational evaluation of their photographic function in 1965, and another challenging exercise was held in Louisiana later that year. However, strategic reconnaissance remained the province of SAC's specialist RB-47 family, U-2s and (from 1965) SR-71s. During LeMay's years in command SAC had lost at least 13 large reconnaissance aircraft in covert Cold War operations, ten of them being piston-engined RB-29s or RB-50s, but the attraction of using a supersonic type for these hazardous missions was not strong enough to generate more contracts.

CHAPTER FOUR

INTO SERVICE

B-58A 59-2456 with four B43 shapes and a TCP aboard in April 1961. The chosen format for the wing and engines ruled out the carriage of drop tanks, so all fuel had to be contained internally and in the main pod. The various pods were integral to the design from the outset and manufactured in the same production facility. Pods tended to assist directional stability in flight (*Terry Panopalis Collection*)

The B-58's fortunes peaked in July 1959 as the B-47s began to show their age and the promise of the XB-70 had waned. At that stage SAC planned five bombardment wings, each with three squadrons of fifteen Hustlers. As costs rose B-58A orders continued to shrink, and by December 1960 it was clear that only 148, later reduced to 116, would be built (including the 30 pre-production examples), rather than the 290 B-58A/Bs anticipated in July 1959. The last aircraft was delivered, to the 305th BW, on 26 October 1962.

SAC commander Gen Thomas Power had intended to form three B-58 wings, with activation of a third wing and its attendant KC-135A tankers at Little Rock, Arkansas, already initiated when cuts in the production run scuppered this plan. Instead, the lifespan of its predecessor, the B-47, was extended within at least one SAC wing. Comments to the effect that the B-58, at $26.7m a copy (including development costs), was more than worth its weight in gold, while containing an element of truth, became mantras for opponents of the programme – as did the reports of two-day maintenance periods between flights.

Nevertheless, in 1960, SAC was still committed to forming two B-58A bombardment wings, and the deterrent effect of even small numbers of Mach 2 bombers was seen to be strategically worthwhile in forcing the Soviet Union to invest heavily in new defences, as they had done for the B-52 threat.

The first Hustler wing, the 43rd BW, commanded by Col James Johnson, moved from Davis-Monthan AFB, Arizona, to Carswell AFB on 15 March 1960. The unit had received its first 12 aircraft at a ceremony on 23 December 1959. At Carswell it replaced the 7th BW (with B-36s), the wing also taking over the tasks of the 3958th OETS, which had conducted pre-service trials from 1 March 1958. Further aircraft began to arrive from the adjacent Fort Worth plant in March and August 1960, including the first TB-58A (55-0670) to help fulfil the wing's duties as SAC's Hustler training unit. The aircraft would undertake this important role alongside TF-102A Delta Daggers that were present expressly for that purpose.

The 43rd's full complement was 40 aircraft, including 11 that had been through the *Flash-Up* modification and standardisation process. Like the 7th BW before it, the 43rd had the advantage of operating within a very short distance of the aircraft's manufacturer, although its operational readiness was still impeded for some time by maintenance and spare parts problems.

Carswell's Hustler wing had a distinguished history in heavy bombing, seeing combat in the South West Pacific Area with B-17 Flying Fortresses (including participation in the Battle of the Bismarck Sea in March 1943) and B-24 Liberators as part of the Fifth Air Force. Equipped with the B-29 Superfortress in November 1947, the unit started to receive brand new B-50s just three months later – one of these aircraft made the first non-stop round-the-world flight in 1949. The 43rd switched to the B-47E in 1954 and became operational with the B-58A in July 1962. Its trio of medium bomb squadrons were the 63rd, 64th and 65th BS(M)s.

In 1964 the 43rd BW moved to Little Rock AFB, which would have accommodated the third B-58 wing had it been formed, and was already home to a major SAC Titan II missile complex. In September the wing was placed on nuclear alert for the first time. Although SAC policy required aircraft to carry bomb wing identity patches rather than squadron colours, the latter preserved their individuality, as former DSO Howard Bialas recalled. 'Each wing had three squadrons but only one wing staff. There was competition between the squadrons, so I think the SAC plan was best'.

The second wing, the 305th BW, was established in much colder conditions than Carswell's at Indiana's Bunker Hill AFB (re-named Grissom AFB in May 1968 in honour of astronaut Virgil 'Gus' Grissom, lost in the Apollo I capsule fire on 27 January 1967) on 1 February 1961. Commanded by Col Frank O'Brien, it consisted of three twelve-aircraft squadrons, namely the 364th, 365th and 366th BS(M)s. The wing's first aircraft (59-2461, nicknamed *Hoosier Hustler*) arrived on 11 May, and TB-58As were delivered from July to enable IOC to be achieved in September. It reached its full complement of Hustlers in May 1962.

The 305th BW also traced its origins back to World War 2, when it too was equipped with B-17s. Unsurprisingly, SAC commander Gen Curtis LeMay had chosen the wing for a cutting-edge assignment with B-58s as it had been the first USAAF Flying Fortress unit assigned to the Eighth Air Force in England in August 1942. Like the 43rd BW, the 305th went on to operate B-29s from 1950 and B-47s from April 1952, deploying to Europe and North Africa on three occasions.

Bunker Hill AFB also housed its own training school and the EC-135s of the 3rd Airborne Command and Control Squadron from 1966. Their task was to attempt to provide bomb damage assessment after a nuclear strike.

The 305th BW's first batches of crews, with pilots coming mainly from B-47 squadrons, were trained at Carswell's 43rd Combat Crew Training School until its own training unit was activated at Bunker Hill AFB. Training a squadron to full combat-ready standard took up to eight months, and replacement crews were generated at the rate of six annually. SAC chose crews from its most highly qualified personnel, including pilots with a minimum of 1000 hours on jets and navigators with at least 500 hours. The latter initially came from B-36 and B-47 units, and many completed a rapid conversion course at Mather AFB near Sacramento, California. Preparation of DSOs took longer to organise, and the earliest candidates received some instruction from Convair personnel and more from other crew members and manuals. Experienced crews could be considered combat ready after five training missions.

Pilots gained initial experience in the T-33 at Perrin AFB, Texas, to revise instrument flying and in the TF-102A to gain delta wing experience – in many cases their first of that kind. Conversion to the Hustler was easier for pilots with experience of the B-47, and was completed even more quickly if they had flown Convair's delta-wing fighters. Many found that the Hustler handled quite like the TF-102A, and after their two flights in the fighter they would solo in the Delta Dagger with an instructor in an accompanying chase aircraft.

Navigators and DSOs lacking previous experience on B-36s or B-47s had their own basic training courses, also conducted at Mather AFB, that lasted eight and six weeks, respectively. Pilots and DSOs were united quite early in the conversion course, as they would share many of the piloting duties. They studied nuclear weapons delivery together and worked on simulated flights as a team, flying three or four 'missions' of up to four hours' duration in a simulator that could provide pitch, yaw and roll movement to add realism. In an emergency, the DSO had all the checklists and flight manuals in his cockpit for consultation. The pilot would inform him of any worrying indications on the front cockpit instrument panels and the DSO would then look up solutions. The next stage for the would-be Hustler crewmen was to make their first training flight in a TB-58A.

Navigators trained with their own navigation and bombing specialists in a dedicated simulator, joining their allocated crew at the time of their first solo flight in a B-58A. As an integrated crew, they could then fly navigation legs at various altitudes, conduct bombing runs at subsonic and supersonic speeds and gain vital practice in aerial refuelling on flights lasting up to eight hours. After eight solo B-58A flights, more simulator training (with an emphasis on emergency procedures) check flights with a SAC standardisation crew and a series of written examinations, a crew would be considered fit to take charge of a nuclear-armed Hustler. Only then was a crew designator number with an 'R' prefix allocated.

Hustler training programmes involved around two daily flights at each base by TB-58As, with crews making at least seven flights in the training Hustler to add to their 30 hours in the flight simulator, giving them a

B-58A 59-2430 was the second Hustler assigned to the 1960 SAC Bombing Competition at Bergstrom AFB, Texas. Here it wears the markings of the 6592nd TS and 43rd BW, and it was later reassigned to the 305th BW. Draconian security measures were strictly enforced at all SAC bases throughout the height of the Cold War (*USAF*)

total of between 70 and 90 hours of flying time within a 125-hour overall syllabus. Each crew member was a highly-qualified specialist in his own sphere, and there had to be considerable cooperation between them.

In the B-47, there was a co-pilot who was also the radio operator and tail gunner, and in the B-52 a crew could share piloting duties and employ its DSO as radio monitor, assistant navigator and purveyor of recorded music on long flights. Virtually isolated in their own cockpits, the three Hustler occupants dealt separately with defensive electronics, bombing/navigation equipment and piloting systems that were more demanding than those in any previous SAC bomber. However, close crew coordination was essential, and operating the bombing/navigation system's nine modes or the defensive electronics required great concentration by the two crewmen concerned.

The selection process for up to 1500 maintenance personnel for each wing operating the complex new bomber was rigorous, with only the most highly qualified candidates being recommended. Initially they came from B-47 units, and then increasingly from wings flying early B-52s.

Neil Byrd's first operational assignment was to Grissom AFB in 1969 as a specialist in the AFCS. 'Seeing a B-58 up close for the first time, I was impressed with its size, polished sleekness and the fact that it looked "all-business"'. His on-the-job training included, 'sitting in a mock-up of the capsule seat', where he was, 'told of a dent in the ceiling caused by the inadvertent ejection of an airman who did not check the safety pins [with their red streamers] on the ejection handles before climbing in'. The technician was attempting to remove an object from beneath the aircraft's middle cockpit capsule when it fired with him still in its seat.

Pilots like Capt 'Gray' Sowers, who came from Stratojets, found the Hustler easy to fly by comparison – 'You didn't fly the B-47, you had to drive it'. The 43rd BW, as the first to field the Hustler, took on the role of demonstrating its operational strengths and rebutting the criticisms about its range and endurance. Lt Col Legge and Capts Andrew Rose and Ray Wagener flew 55-0671 for 11,000 miles at an average speed of 620 mph on a 23 March 1960 flight that took 18 hrs 10 min – a long-standing record for the type. The Hustler remained on autopilot for 15 hours, with only slight 'stick jitter' being noticed by the crew. There were some problems with the air conditioning and cabin pressurisation, but the main source of discomfort was that the crew had consumed all their liquid refreshment within the first 12 hours.

Only two aerial refuelling sessions were required, one to transfer 87,000 lbs of fuel and a second to take on 60,000 lbs. When the aircraft landed, two of the engines still had full oil tanks and the Nos 1 and 2 engines had only used two quarts each. Convair base support manager 'Doc' Witchell noted that the same aircraft made five flights of ten hours or more during March, totalling 67 hours in the air. For any remaining doubters it was useful proof of the bomber's ability to conduct SAC's long-range missions reliably.

Participation in the annual SAC bombing competition began in September 1960, only five months into the type's service career. Flying B-58A 59-2429, two Carswell crews – N-01, comprising Maj Henry Deutschendorf (pilot) and Capts William L Polhemus (navigator/bombardier) and Ray R Wagener (DSO), and N-02, consisting of Majs Harold Confer (pilot) and Richard Weir (navigator/bombardier) and Capt Howard Bialas (DSO) – would have won the competition but for minor technical deficiencies that saw them placed fifth overall. However, their scores for radar bombing and navigation were the best in the two-day event, and for one mission the team were on the runway and ready to roll only 2 min 10 sec after receiving the order to scramble. B-58 crews regularly got airborne from a ground-alert posture within five minutes – a better time than any B-52 squadrons could achieve at that point.

DSO Howard Bialas described the 1960 event for this volume;

'It was one mad scramble, with only six weeks between becoming combat ready and the competition. I was originally on crew N-01, but was switched to N-02 in May 1960. We knew we had to be the first one to launch as we would overtake any "BUFF" [B-52] due to our higher cruising speed. When the klaxon sounded we were in the BOQ [Base Officers' Quarters] area, "resting and guessing". We were driven to the aircraft by a major, I think, observing speed limits.

'Timing started when we crossed the line in front of the plane. Dick Weir ran to check the weapons safety switch on the pod, while Hal Confer and I raced up the steps and slid into our stations. Pre-cocking of the plane meant inboard throttles advanced to the starting position, radio switches on, instrument power on. The groundcrew cranked the electrical cart and the air start cart, which cranked both inboard engines of the plane. While Confer was starting the other two engines Weir and I were copying the launch message, decoding it, cross-checking it and, when we had agreement, shouting "Go!" We then got strapped in. Confer moved the aircraft forward five feet when advised by the line crew that the electrical connection and air cart were clear and chocks removed. We were delayed several minutes while waiting for the rest of the competitors to crank and taxi.

'The first item was air refuelling. We had an inadvertent disconnect, otherwise all was well, so we entered the navigation leg [of the route]. Just minutes prior to completing it the in-flight printer [IFP], which recorded the aircraft's position, failed, so we lost the navigation leg.

'Turning towards Atlanta, my fuel computation was running on track or a little better than expected, so we started the acceleration to Mach 1.5 and a climb to 45,000 ft a few minutes early despite the No 1 engine's afterburner refusing to light – I had experienced the same problem in my first flight in the Hustler. Our maximum speed was limited to Mach 1.5 with only three afterburners working. Between changing some fuses and trying to get the IFP and afterburner to work (which required peeling off my parachute harness and safety belt), I was three seconds late on scoring my defensive jamming run. The ground radar gents took the blame, stating that they had just changed recording devices. Between monitoring UHF and HF radios, the interphone and also trying to do in-flight maintenance, I was nearly overwhelmed.

'We reached 46,000 ft and Mach 1.5 seconds before Weir initiated the "bombs away" tone. The aircraft literally gave up and descent was rapid into the low-level starting point. A spring in the radar tracking handle broke and each time Weir gave a new heading to the Pilot Direction Instrument, Confer tried to follow. That was a wild ride.

'We entered the low-level route in total darkness, using dead reckoning for navigation. I gave Confer headings and timed distances to the next turns with a stopwatch while Weir tried to figure out what his equipment problem was. We felt a loud thump and thought Confer had hit a pine tree, but the plane kept flying and no alarms sounded so we pressed on. Our low-level target was Joplin, Missouri. Weir shouted, "I got it", so Confer climbed from 500 ft to 2500 ft for simulated weapon release.

'The night low-level leg was a thrill for us, as practice flights were normally restricted to 450 knots, but we were flying at 550 knots at an altitude of 500 ft. The "bombs away" tone was very brief. Confer continued to climb to 35,000 ft. As we passed south we could see Dallas/Fort Worth and discussed just going home to Carswell, but then remembered that our clothes were in Austin, Texas.

'After engine shut-down we delayed opening our hatches, thinking we had blown the whole mess, but the groundcrew were pounding on them with bottles of cold refreshment. The bombing scores had been posted and we were the winning crew!'

By 1962, now-Lt Col Richard Weir had become Chief of Bombing and Navigation for the 43rd BW, briefing crews on their radar bombing range targets before they set off on practice missions to Matagorda Island or the Laurel, Mississippi, range areas. A computer scoring system calculated the distance of each simulated bomb from the target. Miscalculations by the crew or their equipment ended up on the 'Bad Bomb Board'.

HUSTLING RECORDS

In 1960, conscious that it now possessed a record breaker, SAC decided to make some very public demonstrations of the B-58's spectacular performance. By October 1963 the aircraft had duly secured an extraordinary total of 19 official world records.

Two of these came during the course of Project *Quick Step*, undertaken at Edwards AFB in January 1961 using 43rd BW B-58A 59-2442 *Untouchable*. The bomber lived up to its nickname by breaking three world speed-with-payload records over a 1242-mile closed-circuit course. Maj Deutschendorf (father of singer John Denver and the first SAC pilot to fly the B-58) and his former SAC bombing competition crew achieved 1061.8 mph – more than 361 mph faster than the previous record-holder, Col Edward Taylor, who had set his time in an RF-101C Voodoo on 8 April 1959. Their aircraft carried 4409 lbs of ballast to meet the payload requirements that specified loads of zero, 1000 kg and 2000 kg for the record attempts.

Majs Elmer Murphy and Eugene Moses and 1Lt David Dickerson look over the route of their 10 May 1961 Blériot Trophy flight in 59-2451 *The Firefly*. Sadly, the aircraft with this crew crashed and all were killed on take-off from Le Bourget two weeks later (*Terry Panopalis Collection*)

Maj Harold Confer's 43rd BW crew, also 1960 SAC bombing competition winners, similarly became triple record-breakers in the speed-with-payload stakes, flying a zero payload, 1000 kg and 2000 kg on 14 January 1961 – 48 hours after Deutschendorf's flight. Their speed over the same closed-circuit course was 1284.73 mph, which was more than twice that of the previous record set by a Soviet crew in 1957. The flight in 59-2441 *Road Runner* earned Confer and his crew the Thompson Trophy, this prestigious prize having never previously been won by a bomber crew.

In May 1960 the 43rd BW had become permanent holders of the Blériot Trophy, established by Louis Blériot in 1930 for a flight that could sustain a speed above 1242.74 mph for more than 30 minutes. When pioneer aviator Blériot had set his criteria for the winner of the trophy, the speed required had probably seemed an unrealistic target. However, Majs Elmer Murphy and Eugene Moses and 1Lt David Dickerson averaged 1302.07 mph for the prerequisite 30 minutes over a 669.4 miles course, guided by their AN/ASQ-42V system.

A further headline-grabbing French connection was made on 26 May 1961 when Maj William Payne, with Capt Polhemus and Wagener, flew B-58A 59-2451 *The Firefly* to the Paris Airshow, setting two new records in so doing. Their New York to Paris time was 3 hrs 19 min 58 sec (about the same time as the Concorde airliner would subsequently take over that route on a daily basis from 1977) for an average speed of 1089.36 mph, and their Washington, DC to Paris time over 3833.4 miles was 3 hrs 39 min. Including the first leg from Carswell, the crew's journey totalled 5150 miles in less than six hours, with an aerial refuelling near Greenland. Their exploits earned the 43rd BW both the Mackay and Harmon Trophies for the first supersonic Atlantic crossing, the time set by the Hustler having almost halved the previous record.

The crew of 59-2451 *The Firefly* plan the Washington, DC to Paris flight on 26 May 1961. They are, from left to right, Capts William L Polhemus (bombardier/navigator) and Raymond R Wagener (DSO) and Maj William R Payne (pilot) (*USAF*)

The Firefly's return trip from Le Bourget on 3 June was flown by the Blériot Trophy crew. On take-off,

In-flight refuelling was a crucial factor in lending credibility to the B-58A as a medium/long-range bomber. Here, *Quick Step II* Hustler 59-2451 *The Firefly* takes on fuel from the high-speed boom of a KC-135A on 26 May 1961. On that day, this aircraft set new speed records for flights from New York to Paris and from Washington, DC to Paris, winning the Harmon Trophy in the process (*Terry Panopalis Collection*)

Maj Murphy performed a low-altitude roll as the aircraft entered a low cloud-base, triggering an elevon control problem. This had probably occurred due to a faulty attitude indicator reading, as the jet's stability gyroscope had not run up to speed prior to the roll being flown. Such a manoeuvre, in any case, would have 'tumbled' the navigator's gyro platforms and consequently put the radar and inertial navigation system out of alignment, making recovery from the roll in cloud very difficult. The Hustler crashed into a potato field near Louvres and exploded in a huge fireball, killing all three crew members.

Despite this setback, the record-breaking flights continued. On 5 March 1962 the 43rd BW set a new transcontinental speed record for a non-stop return trip from Los Angeles to New York, beating the time previously set on 25 May 1961 by US Navy crews in F4H-1 Phantom IIs from VF-121 in Project *LANA*. Capt Robert 'Gray' Sowers flew 65th BS/43rd BW B-58A 59-2458 *Cowtown Hustler* with Capts Robert McDonald (navigator) and John T Walton (DSO) at an average speed of 1214.71 mph. Capt Walton subsequently noted;

'We trained for about four months prior to the flight, practising aerial refuelling and things of that nature. The B-58 was a standard production version with no special modifications. The groundcrew waxed and polished the aircraft until it shined, but other than that it was flown like any other mission. The certification folks went over the aircraft with a fine tooth comb. They actually recorded the serial numbers on the engines before we took off so they could check them after we landed and be absolutely certain that the aircraft wasn't switched en route.'

The crew had to refuel three times, once rather unexpectedly. As they approached the official start point of the flight from an entry over the Pacific, 'we accelerated up to Mach 2 and passed directly over the ground station recording the official start time. However, the aircraft was lost in the ground clutter and we got called back because we had not been officially verified. We flew back out to the rendezvous with the tanker and topped off the fuel and flew back over the starting point again'.

The flight was officially dubbed Operation *Heat Rise* because 'we were pushing the ram air temperature above the normal operating limit, approaching the point where the aircraft tended to melt'. They were told that they could exceed the normal maximum skin temperature of 114°C caused by air friction on the skin, but they should not exceed 125°C. Walton reported that at one point they reached 1400 mph – the speed at which that maximum temperature was likely to be reached and honeycomb skin panels could begin to unbond. The extreme heat removed many of the decals and markings from the aircraft. The crew were delayed slightly on one refuelling session by radio frequency overload and the loss of their 50,000-watt magnetron navigation radar transmitter after its antenna ceased to operate.

Ten tankers were needed as two Hustlers were scheduled for the flight, each transferring up to 85,000 lbs of fuel per rendezvous, although one had to drop out at the start of the return trip. The latter, averaging 1081.77 mph in 2 hrs 15 min 50.8 sec, was a 'beat the sun' flight that was faster than the earth's rotating speed relative to the sun. The crew's overall average speed of 1214.71 mph also beat the previous November 1957 Operation *Sun-Run* record of 3 hrs 7 min set by 1Lt Gustav Klatt in an 18th TRS RF-101C Voodoo, and it won both the Bendix and Mackay Trophies for the 43rd BW in 1962. In fact the B-58 became the outright holder of the Bendix Trophy, because it was awarded for the last time that year.

Two more records fell to a Hustler flown by famous USAF test pilot Maj Fitzhugh Fulton, crewed with Capt W Payne and civilian flight engineer C R Haines, on 18 September 1962. B-58A 59-2456 zoom-climbed to 85,360.84 ft with an 11,023-lb payload, beating a previous Soviet-held record and winning the Harmon Trophy for its crew. This particular flight not only showed that the B-58A could be controlled in the descent from such thin atmospheric conditions, it also demonstrated how such a flight might be used to launch a smaller craft to service orbital satellites.

The 305th BW secured the last of the B-58's string of records with a flight from Tokyo to London by Hustler 61-2059 *Greased Lightning* on 16 October 1963 at an average speed of 938 mph. Pilot Maj Sidney Kubesch, with Maj John Barrett and Capt Gerard Williamson, followed Arctic airspace training route *Glass Brick* (which could well have become an operational route in time of war) to the Far East. The jet, along with three other B-58As, flew to Kadena AB, Okinawa, via Andersen AFB, Guam, prior to making its supersonic flight over the Aleutian Islands, Alaska and Greenland at an altitude of 53,000 ft. The aircraft eventually

Famous for its 26 May 1961 world record flight from New York to Paris, *The Firefly* sits on the ramp at Le Bourget under cloudy skies several days after its arrival in France. Following its Paris Airshow appearance, for which the red tail stripes seen here were added, the aircraft was lost in a crash shortly after taking off from the airport on 3 June 1961 (*USAF*)

B-58A 59-2458, winner of the Bendix and McKay Trophies, as seen in 43rd BW service in 1968. The aircraft was fully restored in 1984 for preservation within the National Museum of the USAF at Wright-Patterson AFB (*Terry Panopalis Collection*)

landed in Britain at RAF Greenham Common to signal the end of the longest supersonic flight up to then – the aircraft had spent more than five hours above Mach 1.

Although the crew won five more international absolute records, their time could have been reduced by an hour had one of *Greased Lightning's* afterburners not failed after the aircraft's fifth in-flight refuelling. Shorter times on the same route would be achieved in subsequent years, but Kubesch's flight was the last to be submitted for official international recognition. It was also a powerful indication of the threat posed by SAC's supersonic strategic weapon.

THE MISSION

Despite its revolutionary and complex characteristics, the B-58A had become a dependably functioning element in SAC's grand plan by 1963. This had been achieved thanks to an army of hardworking maintenance technicians like Neil Byrd, who had had to complete intensive training prior to being assigned to either the 43rd or 305th BWs;

'Before I could get to a base with actual airplanes I had to get through six weeks of basic training at Lackland AFB, Texas, and another eight months of technical school at Chanute AFB, Illinois. While tech school was a step up from basic training, we still experienced occasional KP [kitchen patrol] duty and had to march in formation about a mile from our barracks to the training centre.

'Working on the Hustler meant we had to get to grips with some challenging technology. The B-58 used a J-4 gyro package. It consisted of a directional gyro that provided heading information to an instrument in the cockpit. Additionally, it had an option to use a magnetic sensing unit high up in the vertical fin. The usual failure mode of the gyro would be for the [aircraft's] indicated heading to drift from the true heading. For two evenings the same gyro was brought into the shop by the line crew for this drifting problem. Both times I carefully tested it according to the book and it passed. Reluctantly, the line crew re-installed it on the aircraft. The third night I heard, "Hey, Byrd. Your gyro's back!" and this time they rolled it across the room to me. The flat mounting on this otherwise dome-shaped package went "thump-thump-thump" as it came to me. This time it did fail! I got them a new gyro from the store room and there were no further drifting write-ups'.

Maj 'Fitz' Fulton heads the list of flight crew members on *"Ginger's"* (58-0105) undercarriage door, together with 1Lt C R Haines, who was also flight test engineer for Fulton's September 1962 record flight that reached 85,360 ft with an 11,023-lb payload. Their ascent to the cockpit here was obviously made without the usual purpose-built boarding platforms. The last YB-58 to go through the production conversion programme following its long spell at Edwards AFB, the bomber boasts an ARDC shield and Air Force Flight Test Center (AFFTC) titling beneath the cockpit. Following its reworking in 1962, the aircraft emerged in standard SAC markings (*Terry Panopalis Collection*)

After the first year of service life, when up to 30 groundcrew attended to each B-58 at Carswell for training purposes, the size of a regular crew was reduced to around six.

Planning a Hustler mission involved all three crew members, and it started with the completion of a Form 200 (Jet Mission Flight Plan) – a highly detailed spreadsheet that showed the navigation and performance statistics for each leg of the journey. Coordinates, forecast temperatures, ballistics and bomb-release timings were among the myriad of computations required for the Plan. Each crew member had his own folder detailing the navigational and target information, together with classified enemy threat information, that was relevant to his role within the crew.

1Lt David Sharrock, a former high school teacher, was a Combat Intelligence Officer for the 43rd BW at Little Rock AFB from 1967 until the end of B-58 operations at the base, and he 'worked closely with the elite crews who flew that fantastic supersonic aircraft. I worked in the Operations and Plans building next to the Alert Facility. We had 16 fuelled and armed B-58s in the Alert Facility right behind Plans/Ops. Alert crews came in for their mission briefings when they went on seven-day alerts every third week.

'My specific job was to brief an individual three-man crew on the Emergency War Order, which included their flight map and targets should the President order a nuclear strike. I never knew real pressure until I sat with the Wing Commander [Col Sherwin Desens] and other staff as ORI [Operational Readiness Inspection] scores came in. From those crews who flew that fantastic aircraft I learned to "find a way and get it done". I would not trade my time at Little Rock or my association with the aircraft for anything'.

After briefing, a walk-around inspection and checking of the standard Form 781, entry to the cockpits was made from a large purpose-built step-ladder stand that could be wheeled into position by two groundcrew. They would have already opened the three canopies with a control handle in the nose-wheel well. As so much of the airframe could not be reached from ground level, the walk-around was confined to 'readily accessible items' since the groundcrew would have written up a thorough pre-flight report prior to the arrival of the aircrew. However, undercarriage tyres warranted close inspection for cuts or undetected wear.

If nuclear weapons were loaded, a Nuclear Weapons officer and a Nuclear Safety officer were also involved in pre-flight checks. A second, very detailed walk-around check-list was required if smaller B43 nuclear weapons were hung on the four external pylons in addition to the incredibly powerful 30 megaton B53 weapon in the pod.

If the jet was 'cocked' in the alert configuration, prepared and armed for a particular type of mission, the pre-flight check procedure was drastically shortened. A crew would already be assigned to a particular aircraft, and for a practice minimum reaction 'scramble' ordered by SAC HQ, an alert force could be airborne within five minutes. When 'manning the alert', the crew would spend their time out of the B-58 in the nearby 'mole-hole' – an alert facility recessed into the ground within about 300 ft of the aircraft, which were parked in a top-security area fenced by barbed wire and guarded by police with dogs.

As previously noted, the bulky escape capsule hoods restricted access to the cockpits, particularly for larger occupants, although there was room for document briefcases and food boxes. For a DEFCON 1 power-on scramble, an inboard engine would already be running at idle. Only six checklist items were then required, including rather basic ones like 'helmet on' and 'canopy closed', and crews were warned that take-off would not be delayed while checklist items like turning on the oxygen or connecting personal gear were completed. Crews would not know whether they were facing a genuine emergency until they received a coded message on take-off.

During a routine flight, the first 51-item checklist was read through by the pilot and navigator with power off, with a further 26 items run through by the DSO. External electrical power and air conditioning supplies were then connected. Another much longer checklist was then ticked off by all three crew, working with a line groundcrewman over an intercom link. Once completed, the engine starting sequence began using an external air supply cart and electrical power source for all engines, or a cartridge starter in the No 2 engine. The three remaining engines were wound up by bleed air from the second engine, and the process was aided by having the aircraft pointing into the wind. With engines running, the aircraft's electrical and hydraulic systems were checked and engaged, the flight controls tested and all external power sources disconnected.

After yet another checklist run down, the crew was ready to taxi out, keeping the pre-taxi period as short as possible due to the J79's voracious appetite for fuel. Following one last lengthy checklist read-out by the DSO, the bomber commenced taxiing with the engines at around 70 per cent power. Pilots avoided making sharp turns with the nose-wheel steering so as to minimise strain on the eight small tyres for each main-gear unit. For take-off, the afterburners were engaged on brake release, adding 60,000 lbs of thrust overall.

Timing was so precise that the navigator would give the pilot a count-down from 30 seconds to take-off so that he could increase the power and go into afterburner five seconds before the allotted take-off

The 43rd BW chose a particularly athletic crew to demonstrate an alert 'scramble' in this 1966 image. In August 1964, this particular aircraft, B-58A 58-1011, had become the wing's first operational Hustler, having also been the first jet to pass through the production conversion programme. Note the individual identity number for the MB-1C pod (*Terry Panopalis Collection*)

time, having released the brakes on the exact second. Take-off speeds were computed according to weight, but 190 knots was the usual 'S1 commit' speed at which a take-off could not be aborted. Airspeed checks for take-off were announced to the pilot by the DSO during the 20-second take-off run – one way in which inter-cockpit duties were shared.

'Unstick', with the nose at a 24-degree AoA, was achieved at 203 knots after a ground run of 7850 ft, although this could be significantly extended with a full fuel load and the very high ambient temperature at Carswell AFB. With summer temperatures exceeding 100°F, the aircraft often needed all 13,000 ft of the base's runway. The initial climb speed for a loaded aircraft was a fighter-like 17,000 ft per minute, so the landing gear had to be raised immediately after take-off. Initial climb rate was 350 knots, at which point afterburner would be disengaged and the aircraft would continue to climb at 425 knots to reach Mach 0.9.

The autopilot was then engaged in the required mode, and it would keep the aircraft to its flight-plan. Its controls were located near the throttle levers in the pilot's cockpit so that he could use them without having to release the control column. Control of the autopilot could be passed to the navigator, who could select manual steering using a miniature control column (or 'tracking and flight controller unit') on his lower right panel. Bank angles in that case were limited to 30 degrees.

A normal cruise speed of 525 knots was preferred, but this could rise to 600 knots at sea level or 1147 knots at 40,000 ft. In normal cruise the J79 engines were running at 9700 lbs thrust, rising to 15,500 lbs in afterburner, which could be maintained for over an hour. Maximum speed was determined partly by the airframe's highest permissible skin temperature. This had to be monitored with skin gauges, and it was set at 115°C. It could, however, rise to 125°C before structural damage was likely.

The navigator, who was often considered to carry the greatest responsibility both before and during a mission, controlled the analogue ballistics computer and weapons release panel. The latter had an emergency electric weapons release switch and a stand-by mechanical release handle to activate the pod's pneumatic dropping system if there was an electrical failure.

For most of the Hustler's flights in service, the radar bomb score (RBS) was used rather than real ordnance. This device transmitted a tone signal to a ground RBS site until the point of simulated bomb release, when the tone stopped. An ink trace on a plotting board recorded the radar track up to that point and then the accuracy of the simulated bomb run and drop would be calculated, allowing for the time of release, type of weapon and wind data. One of Carswell's most-used RBS sites was in St Louis, Missouri, where a mobile radar on a hilltop could track the B-58s' bombing runs as they approached from various directions, avoiding the crowded commercial air routes. For the bomb-run, from the initial point (IP) onwards the aircraft was flown by the navigator using his side-mounted control stick connected to the autopilot and bombing/navigation system.

A comprehensive AN/ASH-17 air navigation data recording system stored information from all the aircraft's computer and navigation systems for analysis after a mission and printed it on a paper roll or presented it as a photograph. It also recorded data from the AN/ASH-15 bomb damage evaluation system. RBS runs along a 75-mile track were made repeatedly, with the jet completing up to eight passes per sortie over a radar scoring site.

The B-58's relatively short combat range by SAC standards – the main source of criticism in respect to its performance – necessitated frequent aerial refuelling, usually at 30,000 ft. This was only possible with flying boom-equipped KC-135As which passed fuel to the Hustler through a receptacle just ahead of the windscreen. When the doors over the receptacle were opened, they revealed an illuminated slipway that acted as a guide for the tanker's 'boomer'. Fuel then flowed through a manifold into the reservoir tank, and from there to the main internal tanks and the pod tanks, if they were also selected. The fuel from the reservoir tank, nearest to the cg, was used last. In rough atmospheric conditions an automatic disconnect function would operate to avoid damage if the flying boom's structural limits were exceeded.

As the target approached and the crew received a 'GO' code to proceed with the final stage of their Armageddon mission, all three of them fixed their aluminium-coated silicone rubber thermal window curtains in place with Velcro tape or snap fasteners. The pilot was still allowed a little forward vision through a zip-fastened panel. Weapons and warhead control switches were unlocked and the selector switch for the former was set for a pod or small weapons. With target coordinates and elevation set, the function selector switch was turned to BOMB and the bomb damage evaluation and radar photo switches were activated. A countdown from 200 seconds was then given, with the final ten seconds counted out. Bomb release, or activation of the radar bombing system if the mission was for training, then followed.

B43 'small weapons' weighing 2100 lbs had a ready-safe switch as part of their arming and fusing procedure that gave an R indication for ready and S for safe, initiated by the pilot's arming control switch. In the 'ready' position, the weapon's electrical circuitry armed and fused it ready to be released by high-pressure gas. Two hooks were then retracted and an electrical impulse from the primary navigation system sent the fearsome load on its way, stabilised by its four tail fins and retarded by a parachute that was released from its tail section. Bomb release was monitored mainly by the navigator, who would be watching for the weapon release lamp to illuminate. The system then 'stepped' automatically to the next weapon.

The mechanics of delivering the much larger 36,087-lb MB pod were not significantly more complex than those for the small 'nuke', and they were usually performed by using the autopilot to minimise the stability changes caused by separating from such a massive external load. An MB pod was held on the lower fuselage by three pneumatically-operated hooks and there were also automatic disconnection points for the supply lines for fuel, electrical circuits and compressed air between the bomber and its burden.

The pod's 57-ft length was divided into compartments for fore and aft fuel tanks, an equipment bay in the nose (used for the KA-56 camera in the LA version) and a munitions bay in which ballast would be loaded in the absence of a nuclear warhead. If it had tail fins installed, an MB or LA pod or lower TCP component had to be released before any small weapons were dropped.

The two-component TCP (BLU-2B) required more complex actions in the cockpits. The lower (BLU-2B) section, with a loaded weight of 26,000 lbs, could be jettisoned once its fuel had been transferred to the main aircraft fuel system, although the resulting movement in cg to the rear of the B-58 and the sudden weight reduction caused immediate pitch-up and adversely affected longitudinal stability. The latter, therefore, had to be managed by the automatic fuel system that maintained the cg at a set point.

These issues occurred with the dropping of either type of TCP, and cg problems were even more acute if a pod had to be dropped with fuel still inside. If the cg at that point was too far forward and it was not possible to correct this by moving fuel around the tanks, severe structural damage could occur to the aircraft, particularly at high Mach numbers. The rear fuselage ballast tank was key to successful positioning of the cg.

Like the MB pod, the lower TCP section was released by gas pressure activated by switches in either the pilot's or navigator's cockpits. The upper pod (BLU-2B-3) was held in place by the same three hooks that supported an MB pod, which had a similar internal structure for fuel and munitions and was released in the same way. A retractable lower stabilising fin was extended automatically when the release locking pin was disengaged prior to a drop. When the TCP left its carrier, the pilot had to move his control column forwards to counteract the cg change while fuel was moved around to compensate. The lower pod pitched downwards on release, assisted by a 'kicker' charge at the top of its vertical tail fin. A connecting 'pogo' strut held the lower component clear of the fuselage to stop it from rearing up and causing damage as it fell away. A back-up mechanical release handle was provided in case of electrical failure.

After pod release, the Hustler would zoom-climb to more than 50,000 ft at Mach 2 or exit the target area at minimum altitude at Mach 0.92 if the situation favoured a low-level escape. The B-58's small size and high speed made it a difficult target for hostile radar at low altitude, and the bomber's very effective ECM increased its chances of leaving enemy airspace intact – but only if it had not been immolated in the nuclear blast from another bomber or missile.

For the DSO, the mission involved monitoring his MD-7 for fighter threats, his AN/ALR-12 radar warning equipment, his AN/ALE-16 chaff dispenser and AN/ALQ-16 programmable ECM.

With an LA-1 camera pod in place, B-58A 60-1112 is plugged in to ground electrical power and its complex boarding platforms are in place ready for the crew. It served with both the 43rd BW (here) and the 305th BW. Apart from a KA-56 camera and its air conditioning system, the LA-1 pod was little more than a huge fuel tank. Canopy hatches, operated by nitrogen pressure, were not to be opened in headwinds above 60 knots. On the ground, they were usually closed as soon as possible after the crew was in place, partly to suppress the 110-decibel howl of four idling J79s (*USAF*)

As unofficial communications officer, he was also responsible for the AN/APN-135 I-band rendezvous beacon that sent a coded message for a tanker's radar to interrogate to establish contact, position and identity prior to a refuelling session. His cockpit also had controls for the AN/APN-136 J-band position-indicating beacon that was used to establish where the B-58 was relative to other aircraft. Finally, it was also generously supplied with various circuit breakers, which he might have to pull if so instructed by the pilot.

As if dealing with all of this equipment was not enough, the DSO also had to monitor the fuel system – a key job in the thirsty B-58 – in his role as de facto co-pilot. Using his special slide-rule (calibrated for the different types of pod that could be carried by the Hustler), he had to calculate whether the aircraft's critically important cg was correctly positioned at its intended speed, allowing for external bomb loads, the type of pod being carried, chaff, flares and ammunition, as well as the fuel. This had to be done every 15 minutes at supersonic speed to back up calculations by the on-board computer.

Landing the Hustler was an exacting process that required different techniques from a conventional aircraft, as the delta wing meant that there was no clearly defined stall point and it had no flaps or conventional ailerons or elevators. Pilots worked with graphs showing minimum flying speeds at predetermined weights, altitudes and AoA, with the latter not exceeding the normal maximum of 17 degrees. For landing, the unusually steep 16-degree AoA obviously restricted the pilot's forward view.

Landing speed was controlled with the throttles, knowing that a one per cent change in engine rpm could alter the sink rate on approach by 400 ft per minute. Merely increasing power would not reduce the sink rate unless the nose was also lowered slightly – a peculiarity of the delta wing format. Pilots were warned that excessive use of 'up' elevator, which would rapidly increase lift and AoA in a normal 'tailed' aircraft, could have the opposite effect with a delta and increase the sink rate. Lowering the nose slightly induced extra speed that had to be lost before touch-down at 190 knots.

Prior to landing, the normal rate of descent was 150 ft per minute at a typical weight of 63,100 lbs (assuming that weapons had been released) and 200-210 knots, with the nose at 12.5 degrees for the descent from 50 ft. Even at this reduced AoA, the pilot could not see ahead along the runway until he briefly lowered the nose after touch-down to check his alignment with the tarmac. The nose was then raised to 16°AoA exactly to make full use of aerodynamic braking.

Deployment of a drag parachute before touchdown (almost a normal procedure with the B-47, which had a 16-ft diameter parachute to control approach speeds and a main braking parachute since it was so reluctant to decelerate) was not permitted, although the B-58's 'chute was released on touch-down. The parachute would separate automatically if the aircraft accelerated beyond its set deployment speed of 160 knots in case the pilot had to attempt a 'go-around' second landing. The nose was then lowered when speed dropped to 100 knots and full-up elevator was applied, as well as wheel braking, for a typical ground roll of 2580 ft. The B-58's landing speed – comparatively high for a SAC aircraft – was critical, for every ten knots above the calculated speed added up to 1000 ft to the landing run.

The highly-polished surface of 58-1018 reflects its glamorous (but unidentified) visitor, who is 'holding hands' with *REDDY KILOWATT*, a reference to a cartoon character created by American inventor and marketer Ashton Budd Collins in 1926 to promote US electricity generation – which it did for more than seven decades. After use as a test platform for the B-58's ECM systems, this aircraft was the eighth to go through operational conversion for service with the 43rd BW (*Terry Panopalis Collection*)

The anti-skid system worked at speeds below 25 knots, but it would not stop a wheel with a flat tyre from skidding. With the chances of a blow-out significantly increased with prolonged use of the brakes, even when applied lightly, pilots were repeatedly told during training to use aerodynamic braking and the brake parachute, as well as the full length of the runway. Aerodynamic braking combined with wheel braking was shown to be almost as effective as using the latter in conjunction with the braking parachute.

Heavy braking, even at speeds below 25 knots, could cause tyre damage and overheating of the wheel brakes to the point where there was a serious risk of them exploding. Should a jet return to the flightline with overheating brakes, groundcrew were forbidden from approaching the landing gear for more than an hour after touchdown. The maximum temperature within the brakes was not reached until about 15 minutes after the aircraft had stopped, and they always required a four-hour cooling period, surrounded by wire 'cooling off' protective cages, before their energy-absorbing capacity was restored and they were ready for another landing.

In an emergency, runway barrier engagements were possible at speeds of up to 150 knots using a BAK-11 or BAK-12 barrier system, and this was tested with both types of pod still aboard the Hustler. Brake tests by YB-58A 58-1020 included aborted take-off runs at weights of up to 163,000 lbs and with shields fitted over the undercarriage units, generating forces that reached 18 million foot-pounds per brake unit at speeds of up to 131 knots.

CHAPTER FIVE

GLOBAL REACH

SAC frequently ordered no-notice mass scrambles like this one by 305th BW Hustlers at Bunker Hill AFB in July 1965. Crews were not told whether it was a real emergency, but on most occasions the exercises ended before the bombers reached the end of the runway. Although B-58s were limited to only two wings, they comprised more than 12 per cent of the SAC bomber fleet by 1967 (*Terry Panopalis Collection*)

In an attempt to improve the B-58A's credibility within SAC in 1960, Convair tried to capitalise on the Hustler's quicker response time while on ground alert compared with the dominant B-52 force. The bomber was also proposed for the airborne alert role as an alternative to the longer-ranging Boeing aircraft. From 1958, SAC's answer to the growing Soviet threat (particularly after the Cuban Missile Crisis of October 1962) was to keep a proportion of its bomber force airborne 24 hours a day. They were nuclear-armed and ready to enter hostile airspace in time to counter an enemy attack with minimal delay before any SAC bases could be destroyed by missiles.

Originally the proportion of bombers to be airborne at any one time was set at an ambitious 25 per cent, or around 150 aircraft. At the B-58 bases during the Cuban Missile Crisis, 20 aircraft were armed with all five 'nukes' and on five minutes ground alert. However, for the rest of the decade, only ten or twelve were maintained in this state of readiness. At Carswell, crews stood alert for seven days on alternate weeks. Meanwhile, B-52s flew *Steel Trap* and *Chrome Dome* missions, completing flights on routes to the Mediterranean and north of Alaska that could last more than 24 hours and cover in excess of 10,000 miles.

Although the B-58's airborne alert endurance was inferior to the B-52's, Convair hoped that the bomber's considerably quicker speed to a target from orbits near the enemy's borders would convince SAC to buy more

Hustlers. Unfortunately for the company, it did not. However, the aircraft was better suited than the B-52 to the low-altitude scenario that was forced upon SAC by improved Soviet defences.

Although the G- and H-models of the B-52 were essentially redesigned for low-altitude penetration, their airframes encountered severe fatigue problems. There were no such issues with the B-58 thanks to its much smaller, stiffer delta wing, which proved to be more resilient in rough air conditions below 500 ft. The pilot's cockpit area was also relatively free of external turbulence. Indeed, Hustler crews found their low-altitude missions at 600 knots and 500 ft far more exhilarating than Mach 2 flights at 50,000 ft, where the only indication of their speed was to be seen on the Mach meter.

The aircraft's stability and better resistance to turbulent weather conditions made it a more comfortable ride than a big-wing B-52 at low altitude. However, turbulence at 200 ft and 600 mph could still make things quite uncomfortable, rendering cockpit instruments hard to read. Additional friction from the denser air at lower altitudes also increased the temperature in the cockpit. Convair received funding to improve the aircraft's flying controls for low-level flight and to install a terrain-following radar that could be used manually or connected to the autopilot for automatic operation. That radar would have been installed in a pod under the left inboard wing, but the idea was not pursued. Crucially for its self-preservation, the Hustler had a far smaller radar signature than the B-52.

Hustlers of the 43rd BW lined up at Carswell AFB in 1963. In the foreground is 58-1016, the third YB-58A to complete production conversion modifications. It was lost in a hard landing at Little Rock AFB on 20 May 1965, pilot Capt Ralph Semann and DSO 1Lt Ronald Smetek surviving the incident but bombardier/navigator Capt Steve Kichler perishing in the crash. Aircraft 59-1441, second in the row, won the Thompson Trophy as *Road Runner* for its crew, setting six speed records in January 1961 (*USAF*)

EARLY ATTRITION

The aircraft's early safety record, with six major fatal accidents in its first 10,000 hrs of SAC service, improved markedly thereafter. However, the losses sustained in the early 1960s nevertheless resulted in the deaths of six crew members. B-58A 58-1020, the tenth aircraft to go through the production standardisation re-work line, was the first operational loss. A fuel manifold ruptured in flight on 27 December 1961, causing fuel starvation and engine flame-out. Less than two months later, on 15 February 1962, a 43rd BW crew had to eject near Lawton, Oklahoma, from B-58A 59-2447 *RAPID RABBIT* when the flight control system developed a Mach trim problem. Again, the crew survived by ejection during an inverted spin, although the pilot, Maj John Irving, was injured due to a loose seat harness.

The occupants of 43rd BW aircraft 59-2459 were not so fortunate on 5 March 1962 when a severe flight control system failure caused the jet to crash on take-off from Carswell, killing Capts Robert Harter and Jack Jones and 1Lt James McKenzie. The latter had managed to successfully eject, only to land in the blazing wreckage. All B-58s were grounded for a month while the cause was investigated. Navigator Capt Duane Hickey was the only casualty in the crash of 59-2462 following another flight control system failure near Bunker Hill AFB on 12 April 1962.

A similar sequence of failures caused 305th BW aircraft 61-2057 to break up during a supersonic run on 14 September 1962, the aircraft yawing violently until it was effectively travelling sideways at almost Mach 2. Its pod and tail assembly both broke away and the rest of the airframe disintegrated. All three crewmen, Lt Col John Trevisani and Capts Arthur Freed and Reinardo Moure, were killed. Travelling at such extreme speeds obviously left no time to try and deal with any flight control or engine problems, with catastrophic consequences for the crew. At a more mundane, but equally lethal, level, a hard landing at Bunker Hill destroyed 61-2063 on 26 August 1963, and pilot Maj William Brandt was the only survivor.

Another near fatality occurred during a simulated bomb-run by a 305th BW aircraft, the Hustler being intercepted by an ADC F-106A travelling at Mach 2. As the fighter approached from the rear, the bomber's right main undercarriage suddenly extended. Although its doors were ripped away and control problems ensued, the Hustler crew managed to return their aircraft to Bunker Hill, leaving the F-106A pilot perplexed at this unorthodox method of rapid deceleration and evasion.

There were some circumstances in which even the complex Stanley capsule could not save aircrew. Nuclear-armed B-58A 60-1116 was taxiing out at Bunker Hill for a minimum interval take-off (MITO) exercise on 8 December 1964 when the left main wheels hit a metal electrical installation at the edge of the runway. Unable to see the obstruction, pilot Capt Leary Johnson assumed they had rolled into some mud and gunned the throttles. The extra strain collapsed the left undercarriage, fuel gushed from a ruptured wing tank and a conflagration broke out.

Although fully aware that the escape capsule was not rated for ground speeds below 100 knots, navigator Capt Manuel 'Rocky' Cervantes realised that the fire would reach his cockpit first so he ejected. The capsule rocketed him 400 ft up into the air before he landed heavily in a snowdrift, a lack of insufficient forward speed preventing his main parachute from opening. Cervantes died an hour later. Johnson and DSO Capt Roger L Hall abseiled down ropes from the blazing wreck and ran clear before the aircraft exploded.

A second accident on 14 June 1967 revealed another parachute deployment problem. Maj Clint Brisendine was flying B-58A 61-2061 over Lipscombe County, Texas, when his windscreen was damaged by a violent hail storm. He closed his capsule doors and continued to steer the aircraft, although he could not use the throttles. Knowing that he could not 'de-capsulate', he gave the order to eject. Brisendine and DSO Capt Gary M Cechett escaped successfully, but navigator Capt William R Bennett perished when the automatic deployment system failed on his main parachute and a fault in the manual deployment mechanism meant that he could not use that either prior to hitting the ground.

Undercarriage problems persisted into the mid-1960s. B-58A 60-1121 lived up to its *Can Do* nickname on 10 September 1964 when the jet's right undercarriage collapsed on touch-down at Carswell AFB.

A 305th BW B-58A is towed from its 'Hustler Hut' alert barn at Grissom AFB in July 1968. Without a pod attached to its belly, a hangared B-58A usually had a compensating 4000-lb weight attached to its forward pod support to maintain cg. Unweighted Hustlers with no pod and unbalanced internal fuel did tip onto their tails on a few occasions. In flight, a pod-less Hustler had fighter-like acceleration and manoeuvrability, but for landing the crew had to ensure that enough fuel was in the forward tanks to keep the cg ahead of the main undercarriage (*Terry Panopalis Collection*)

After momentarily righting itself, the bomber dipped its right wing and the outer nacelle began to scrape along the runway in a stream of sparks. The pilot's canopy hatch was jettisoned, closely followed by the other two, as the hectic slide continued, with sparks trailing from both right engine nacelles. With the wing and nacelles flexing dangerously, the aircraft finally lurched to a stop on the grass runway border. The navigator exited fast, using his escape rope, and he ran ahead of the crash while the other crew men remained standing in their cockpits (the pilot throwing his helmet down onto the grass) as the emergency vehicles and fire-suppressant helicopter closed in. There was no fire and the B-58 was repaired for another five years of service.

Accidents declined in number for the 305th BW after 1965, with only 59-2437 being lost during that time. Another victim of the B-58's fragile undercarriage, the Hustler had a cylinder in the right main landing gear fail on take-off. The crew (Maj George Tate and Capts Ray Walters and Mosson) had to manage a landing with a partially collapsed right gear leg. All survived, but the aircraft, although substantially intact, was not repaired.

Attrition within the 43rd BW remained high, however, with no fewer than seven Hustlers being destroyed in a variety of ways, including pilot error. B-58A 61-2065 (also used by the 305th BW) stalled on take-off from Bunker Hill on 13 November 1967 when the pilot, Maj Galen Dultmeier, on his first solo flight, over-rotated the aircraft and continued to pull back on the control column in an attempt to coax the Hustler aloft. It stalled and crashed, killing the crew (Dultmeier, navigator Capt Ronald Schmidt and DSO Capt Leroy Hanson).

As Col Phil Rowe, a DSO who served with both the 43rd and 305th BWs in the early 1960s, pointed out, 'The B-58 was not a forgiving bird. It demanded full attention. Adherence to strict procedures and keeping the fuel system in proper configuration was critical. So too was not over-stressing the airplane by pulling excessive g-forces. That was so important that restraints on elevon travel, up and down, were imposed by an automatic control mechanism'. A complex check-out of that g-limiting system was a vital part of every pre-flight procedure.

Another aircraft, 60-1119 *City of Kokomo* and its crew (pilot Maj Richard F Blakeslee, navigator Capt Floyd E Acker and DSO Capt Clarence D Lunt) were lost on 12 December 1966 when it suddenly and inexplicably pitched downwards from 500 ft during a low-altitude nocturnal bomb run. Residents of McKinney, Kentucky, were awoken by a massive flash and explosion, and daylight revealed a crater 100 ft wide and 30 ft deep on local farmland.

In other mishaps, 59-2443 *Bye Bye Birdie* undershot its landing upon arriving at Le Bourget on 15 June 1965, killing the pilot, Lt Col Charles

B-58A 61-2053, assigned to the 305th BW, displays its Second Air Force tail flash in 1969. It was used in test drops of a TCP and four small weapons at Edwards AFB in May 1963. When airborne the B-58A, like all J79-powered aircraft, left its distinctive trademark of heavy, black smoke trails when its engines were in military power rather than afterburner. The J79's maximum permissible exhaust gas temperature (EGT) was 1105°F (*Terry Panopalis Collection*)

Tubbs. In the final serious accident to befall the B-58 force, 61-2056 was abandoned on 18 April 1969 near Danville, Illinois, after the crew detected 'suspected systems anomalies'. In only four cases in the aircraft's last four years of service was a mechanical failure blamed for a loss, and one of those Hustlers, 59-2454, was actually returned to airworthiness after being repaired – it had suffered structural failure of the forward fuselage section while taxiing at Little Rock.

The frequent references to the B-58's high accident rate as the reason for its early withdrawal could only be justified by the ten losses between December 1958 and September 1962, when mechanical failure was indeed the principal cause. In all, 26 out of the total production of 116 were destroyed, although as with most highly innovative designs, the majority of these losses occurred during the flight test or service introduction phase.

COMPETITION SUCCESS AND SIOP

The 305th BW scored well when the SAC Bombing Competition was resumed briefly in 1965, winning the awards for Best Overall Single Mission, Best Crew for Navigation and Best Crew for Bombing. This performance also secured the 305th the award of Best B-58 Wing, with it winning four of the ten trophies awarded overall in SAC. For these competitions the B-58 had the advantage of the newly-introduced in-flight printer tape to record the aircraft's altitude, speed and position at all stages of its flight.

During the Cold War, SAC was expected to deploy its aircraft to bases throughout the world, partly so that 'second strike' missions could be flown in the event of a war in which missiles might have destroyed continental American bases in the conflict's opening stages. B-58As would have then

The crew of 59-2455 race to their 43rd BW aircraft for a practice alert take-off at Carswell. Nash Ramblers or Ford Country Sedan vehicles were usually used to take the crew, their flight gear, data and flight plans, briefcases and lunch boxes to the aircraft parking ramp. After a long mission in their restrictive cockpits, crew members often had to be helped to leave their seats. Although its safety benefits were unquestionable, the capsule occupied a lot of cockpit space and offered little comfort on long flights, particularly as it required the occupants of the rear cockpits to sit with their knees hunched up (*USAF*)

been ready to launch in combat configuration with five nuclear weapons – one in a pod and four on underwing pylons. Attacks on several targets would have been scheduled. Guam and Okinawa were crucial in this strategy, with US-based B-58As flying 14.5-hour flights to Guam and then sometimes adding another four-hour leg to Kadena. At the latter base, stocks of fuel, ordnance and parts were available, together with experienced 'forward base' groundcrew to handle the aircraft.

The Hustler's confined cockpit spaces made those extremely lengthy flights uncomfortable experiences. Some flights could last for more than 15 hours, causing painful leg cramps for capsule occupants that necessitated help in exiting the aircraft after landing. Even the B-47 gave most crewmen the opportunity to stretch their legs occasionally – a luxury not available to B-58 aircrew.

In-flight refuelling made such deployments possible, and at least two tanker sessions were required for the flight from the USA to Andersen AFB, with each refuelling adding 7400 nautical miles to the aircraft's range. A favourite technique for a complete 'fill-up' at around 300 knots was to keep the outboard engines (or one inboard engine) in afterburner and adjust speed and position on the boom with the two inboard engine throttles. Pilots were advised to warn the 'boomer' during night refuelling sessions that they were about to engage afterburner to avoid alarming tanker crews who would not be used to afterburning bombers.

The SIOP in place from 1961 to 2003 specified a comprehensive onslaught by all of the US armed forces' offensive nuclear resources in the event of a Soviet attack. For the two Hustler wings, the SIOP strategy would have involved attempting to hit 160 targets. An attack of this kind

B-58A 59-2434 *Cannonball*, seen here serving with the 43rd BW, was the first example to enter the *Flash-Up* programme. Although the two rear cockpits offered limited visibility, the pilot had fairly large transparencies that frequently developed cracks or symptoms of de-lamination between their layers of glass after high-Mach flight. These were tolerated around the edges of the panels, but a replacement was needed if they migrated inwards more than an inch. The windscreen rain removal system was also capable of anti-icing, while the air conditioning could de-fog the transparencies (*Terry Panopalis Collection*)

would also have involved B-47s and B-52s while the faster B-58s would have provided Soviet defences with more challenging targets and required great expense to devise suitable defensive measures against such a strike.

The Hustler's potential strike capability, with five nuclear weapons rather than two carried by most B-52s, increased their role as 'force multipliers'. One USAF estimate credited the B-58 force with more nuclear strike power than the entire USSR at that point. SIOP, which began for the B-47 wings in 1957, required one-third of both B-58 wings to be on alert for ten-day periods at any time, with crews close enough to their jets to be able to take off within 15 minutes. At Bunker Hill there were often 20 B-58s armed and ready on alert.

For high-altitude SIOP missions to a target at a distance of 4275 miles, a B-58A would take off weighing 163,000 lbs (including 96,520 lbs of JP-4 fuel). This would increase to 167,321 lbs after its first aerial refuelling at around 22,500 ft. The aircraft then accelerated to Mach 0.91 and ascended to 46,880 ft, climbing higher and accelerating in fuel-guzzling afterburner to Mach 2 for up to 500 miles as it reached heavily-defended enemy territory. Weapons could be dropped from 55,650 ft at 1147 knots – the aircraft's maximum permissible speed at that altitude. Descent to cruise altitude and a return to Mach 0.91 were then prescribed, giving a potential 1500-nautical-mile return range to try and reach a friendly base.

In the unlikely event of a wholly subsonic mission profile, the distance to the target could be extended to around 5650 nautical miles, although a B-58A could not sustain altitudes above 49,000 ft without using afterburner even after weapon release. However, its ability to sustain Mach 2 flight for up to an hour (fuel permitting) made it a hard target for fighters that could only attain that sort of speed for a few minutes.

By 1963 the B-58A was established as a formidable element in America's nuclear deterrent, and its many record-breaking flights had made the aircraft a focus of public attention. Indeed, President John F Kennedy's last official duty was a visit to Carswell AFB in Air Force One on 22 November 1963 just an hour before his fateful journey to Dallas and his death.

Hustler wings were fully involved in Cold War practice deployments by 1964. Operation *Order Blank* in April of that year took B-52s and B-58s on long flights, hitting simulated targets in Europe, North Africa and Asia at both high and low altitudes. In all cases SAC demonstrated that it could provide aerial refuelling for such large-scale exercises and put all the aircraft over their assigned targets within three minutes of the specified times.

The B-58's chances of survival during wartime were further enhanced by plans to return them to surviving NATO airfields in Europe or others in Canada after a flight across the north polar area if they had insufficient fuel to get back to their US bases. Failing that, crews were advised to resort to their escape capsules over safe territory like western Germany. *Reflex Capability* was the codename for small detachments of SAC aircraft (mainly B-47s until they were progressively replaced by B-52s from 1965) to foreign bases. Hustlers made their first *Reflex* to Zaragoza on 1 July 1963, and others followed to Guam and British bases.

In the USA the Hustler units, like those flying the B-52, also practised MITO exercises in which up to 15 B-58s were launched within 15 minutes in order to get the retaliatory force airborne before Soviet submarine-launched missiles could wipe out SAC's airfields. The feasibility of such massive exercises was initially tested at Edwards AFB in January 1963 with only six aircraft. In operational use, the B-58A's relatively small wingspan enabled the bombers to use both sides of a SAC runway to take off, reducing the time between jets to 15 seconds – a faster performance than the bigger B-52s could manage in a situation where seconds mattered.

Throughout the 1960s, SAC's relentless and frequent no-notice ORIs kept the two B-58 wings at peak efficiency in every detail. In annual, no-notice 'Bar None' exercises, the alert aircraft were launched and then every other airworthy B-58 and tanker had to be prepared and launched too, in groups of 15. Flying was only suspended if cloud ceilings were below 300 ft and visibility was less than 2500 yards.

Alert barracks – the half-buried 'mole-holes' – were built for nuclear alert crews to await their mission in comfort and lighten the stress of always knowing that they could be called to war at a moment's notice. Crewmen spent time monitoring the international news in order to estimate likely tensions that could cause the alert klaxon to send them running to their aircraft from station wagons that followed uninterrupted routes to the flightline with red warning lights flashing. Crews usually spent alternate weeks on alert, with a refresher flight during the 'off' weeks. They had to remain together as a three-man unit at all times, and jokers commented that if one member went to the bathroom they would all have to go. Golf was a leisure possibility, but players had to be followed around the course by a vehicle to scoop them up and enable them to respond to an alert requirement in the prescribed time.

The aircraft were parked in the open or in 'Hustler huts' while their crews had the benefit of bedrooms, recreation rooms with pool tables and television rooms, as well as facilities for planning missions. Practice missions during non-alert periods included high-altitude navigation training runs and low-level simulated 'oil burner' bomb-runs on an RBS site after planning and briefing sessions that could last for up to four hours. In Carswell's case, its RBS site was at Laurel, although crews also flew Mach 2 nuclear simulations at high altitude and supersonic speed over 'targets' on Matagorda Island.

Their real routes and targets in potential wartime situations were already planned and maps prepared for each crew to carry out the specific mission that they had already studied closely. A Hustler's stellar performance, covering around 1000 ft of ground at low-altitude per second, required extreme accuracy in both planning and navigation. Radar film from previous practice missions was useful in locating precise offset aiming points, although the latter had to be based on actual reconnaissance data for SIOP plans.

CHAPTER SIX

OTHER ROLES AND VERSIONS

NB-58 55-0662 in AFFTC markings with the podded GE J93-GE-3 for the XB-70 bomber and F-108A Rapier fighter beneath its fuselage (*Terry Panopalis Collection*)

The Hustler was such an advanced project from the outset that Convair naturally explored many possibilities for capitalising on its costly research and development. These included modifying the aircraft to allow it to perform other roles or for use as a test vehicle for related projects.

One of the earliest was a 1951 proposal for a long-range interceptor version of the basic design, unofficially known as the B-58D. At that time it was thought that large aircraft with heavy missile and fuel loads would be required to reach out and intercept nuclear-armed intruders at a safe distance with nuclear-tipped air-to-air missiles. Avro Canada's 78-ft-long CF-105 Arrow, weighing 69,000 lbs, and a proposed interceptor development of the North American A-5 Vigilante bomber of similar size and weight were examples of this approach. By 1955 the suggested Convair interceptor had grown even larger, and its pod contained a rocket booster motor. The company proposed a version for TAC and an ECM variant, with a reconnaissance B-58A drafted in 1955. All three proposals had been submitted to the USAF by 1956. Convair's design team also drew up plans for an extended B-58 with a revised wing camber and folding wingtips, rather like those of the XB-70 Valkyrie.

The work on an improved, enlarged aircraft led to the proposed B-58B in 1959, which sought to overcome criticism of the Hustler's range. It would have had five pylons for external ordnance, including the WS-138A

(GAM-87 Skybolt) thermo-nuclear missile for which Convair made a bid in 1959. It lost out to Douglas for the development of that weapon, which was duly cancelled by President Kennedy on 22 December 1962 – the same day as its first successful test launch. Skybolt had been intended for the B-52H and Britain's Vulcan fleet from 1964, offering hypersonic speed and a 1000-mile stand-off range.

The B-58B would have also used its stores pylons for conventional weapons, and the intended configuration was tested using a B-58A in April 1967. Operation *Bullseye* at Eglin AFB, Florida, employed standard multiple ejection bomb racks and ordnance from 750-lb M117s up to 3000-lb M118s. Some 305th BW Hustlers (including 61-2055) flew test sorties with other TAC jets as both strike and pathfinder lead aircraft. In the latter role they were used in much the same way as RB-66 Destroyers would be in Vietnam, with their sophisticated navigational systems providing more accurate guidance to crews of F-4s and F-105s. Some Hustlers performed test missions during *Bullseye* as lone strikers while others operated in formation with dissimilar types. In 1967 it seemed likely that the latter tactic, using B-58s as pathfinders for F-105s, could be utilised for night attacks in Vietnam.

Multiple weapons drops by three B-58As, including 59-2435 *SHACKBUSTER*, in 1961-62 paved the way for trials with conventional weapons in Operation *Bullseye* in 1967. The red score markings on the Hustler's nose represent drops of both nuclear-capable pods and small Class D weapons, while '38' was the aircraft's production number. The first multiple weapons drop was made by Convair crew F J Voorhies, F A Hewes and O D Lively (*Terry Panopalis Collection*)

That capability, using the Hustler's external weapons pylons to carry up to 12 conventional bombs, was also included in the configuration of a simplified B-58A that was offered to the Royal Australian Air Force (RAAF) in 1960 as a Canberra B 20 bomber replacement. The addition of external conventional bombs inevitably increased drag, particularly at low altitude. After protracted consideration of many other types including the British Aircraft Corporation (BAC) TSR.2, the RAAF eventually ordered the General Dynamics F-111C Aardvark. In Britain, the TSR.2's development had been secured after the RAF gave brief consideration in 1956 to the B-58A as a successor to its Canberras. The Hustler's cost, its lengthy flight-test period and apparent lack of conventional low-altitude strike capability at that time ended RAF interest.

Proposals to use the B-58 as a stand-off carrier for ALBMs began in 1957 as an obvious extension of its pod-carrying design. In February 1964 Convair had proposed a joint project with Lockheed to develop a B-58B ALBM launcher. A contract was signed for the launch of four WS-199 aerial ballistic missiles and the first was fired in December 1958 from a B-58A flying at 1100 mph.

The B-58B was cancelled in July 1959, having been succeeded on the drawing board by the even larger B-58C powered by four P&W J58 engines (as used in the Mach 3-capable Lockheed SR-71), two of them moved to the Hustler's wingtips. Weighing more than 200,000 lbs, this 'stretched' Hustler would have carried a wide range of ordnance on strategic, airborne alert and tactical missions at Mach 3, cruising at more than 70,000 ft. Convair also envisaged an interceptor application of this development.

ELECTRIC HUSTLERS

In April 1956 a further podded store was proposed for the high-altitude electronic reconnaissance RB-58A variant carrying a very sophisticated Hughes AN/APQ-69 side-looking airborne radar (SLAR) set that was then under development. Its microwave energy was transmitted at an angle from the side of the aircraft for functions such as terrain mapping. Convair began studies in September 1958 of a Hustler using a SLAR pod containing the Hughes AN/APQ-69 designator set. This technology eventually found application in tactical reconnaissance aircraft.

Its massive pod was very different from the normal MB-1, extending further aft and requiring a different, angular cross-section. The SLAR's size, weight and 50-ft-long antenna would have left no room for fuel within the pod, significantly reducing the Hustler's range and limiting it to subsonic speeds. Although the SLAR pod was flight-tested in 1959, producing satisfactory results at ranges of up to 50 miles, it had in fact been cancelled the previous year like the other dedicated reconnaissance options.

The company's attempts to introduce SAC reconnaissance or ECM Hustlers continued in the late 1950s, despite the 'ferret' ECM system for the aircraft having also been cancelled in May 1958. Its Melpar ALD-4 ECM equipment was used in RB-47s instead, and attrition amongst these specialist aircraft temporarily regenerated interest in an ALD-4-carrying Hustler as a faster alternative in 1960.

However, a USAF request in 1958 for an all-weather reconnaissance system for testing on a B-58A led to Convair asking the Goodyear Aircraft Corporation to submit proposals for suitable equipment in Project *Quick Check*. YB-58 55-0668 *Peeping Tom*, the ninth aircraft to be produced, was converted to RB-58 configuration before eventually becoming a TB-58A. As a YB-58, it was also selected to flight-test the J79-GE-9 engines that would have powered the stillborn B-58B. In June 1958, during the jet's RB-58A period, it was fitted with a *Quick Check* modified MB-1 pod equipped with a Goodyear AN/APS-73 X-Band synthetic aperture radar behind a fibreglass nose radome in a pod that also contained fuel. A Raytheon forward-looking radar was installed in the aircraft's nose within a slightly enlarged radome and a new stellar tracking device was fitted above the navigator's cockpit. Radar imagery was recorded on five-inch film using an AN/GSQ-28 optical signal processor.

Ironically, the B-58A's only operational strategic mission in a conflict situation was a *Quick Check* reconnaissance flight by 55-0668 during the Cuban Missile Crisis. Manned by a Convair/General Dynamics crew, the modified Hustler flew a single ELINT mission along the northern coast of Cuba on 30 October 1962. The AN/APS-73 was effective in providing detailed, all-weather terrain mapping at supersonic speeds over an 80-mile range, and the Cuba flight was duly performed at high-speed. The results achieved with the pod proved to be better at subsonic speeds, however. The *Quick Check* programme was cancelled in late 1962, while the ELINT mission remained with other aircraft types.

PASSENGER PODS

In the mid-1950s, when maximum airspeeds were increasing almost annually, there was a determined effort made by the US aerospace industry to create a supersonic transport aircraft (SST). Convair felt that the company's lead in creating the first relatively large supersonic vehicle should be converted into a civil transport initiative. Although it did not propose a large SST of the size that Lockheed and North American were studying, Convair initially suggested in 1957 that it could convert an MB-1C pod to take five passengers beneath a B-58 and provide some initial experience of commercial supersonic travel. It was also thought that this experiment might promote the idea of rapid transport for crucial military personnel.

Convair then proposed an enlarged, Hustler-based design known as the CV-58-9 that featured the B-58C's four non-afterburning J58 engines and a B-58 wing combined with a fuselage that could accommodate 52 passengers on a Mach 2.4 journey. Outlined in 1960, with a potential in-service date of 1964, the CV-58-9 would have been faster but much smaller than the Anglo-French Concorde, for which the preliminary design studies had begun in 1956.

When the American SST programme received the official go-ahead in April 1961, BAC and Sud Aviation had already completed Concorde designs, using a slender delta wing that originated from prototype work with the Handley Page HP.115 research aircraft and some of the data generated by the Convair XF-92A programme – the latter had, of course, contributed to B-58 development. SST was a response to the potential threat to the US aviation industry posed by Concorde, and it led to design contracts for Lockheed and Boeing, from which the latter's Mach 2.8 Model 2707 was selected for further development. Convair's CV-58-9 was not in the running.

It is conceivable that America's unwelcome experience of supersonic booms, generated mainly by B-58 flights, might have contributed to the US Congress's withdrawal of support for the SST in 1971, when the environmental impact of overland supersonic flight was cited as a major factor in the decision. The Hustler had by then acquired a reputation as the loudest aircraft ever built. In fact, the B-58As' supersonic flights were generally confined to a 1000-mile overwater route between Mobile, Alabama, and a point off the Texas coast near Corpus Christi.

LAUNCHER HUSTLER

NACA's rapid progress in sponsoring a series of X-planes that pioneered supersonic and then hypersonic flight led to a requirement for aircraft that could launch these machines at much higher speeds and altitudes than the piston-engined 'mother ships' used since the 1940s. North American's Mach 6 X-15 was successfully mated with a B-52, and the XB-70 Valkyrie and B-58 were also explored as 'first stage' launchers to boost it sufficiently to reach Mach 6 at sub-orbital altitudes after launch at Mach 3. However, it proved impossible to fit the X-15's vertical fin and wingtips beneath a Hustler. Cancellation of the B-70 in 1961 and a reduction in funding for its NASA use also removed that carrier option.

YB-58 55-0665 became the test-bed for the Hughes AN/ASG-18 fire control system and Mach 6 GAR-9 missile intended for Lockheed's YF-12 fighter, the jet's extended radome earning it the nickname 'Snoopy'. The missile was semi-recessed in a specially-designed pod that also housed a cooling system and telemetry gear. Camera pods were fitted under the outer engine nacelles (*Terry Panopalis Collection*)

The even more adventurous 'Super Hustler' venture in 1958 arose from a CIA request to Convair's head of advanced development, Robert Widmer, for a reconnaissance aircraft that could fly for 4000 miles at a peak altitude of 90,000 ft and avoid radar detection. While the CIA's representative, Richard Bissell, had Lockheed in mind for this extremely demanding task, he gave Convair a chance to produce a rival bid. The initial, complex, proposal would have used a B-58A to carry a second two-component 'Super Hustler' for around 2250 miles towards its target. The parasite machine, manned by two crewmen and powered by a Marquardt ramjet, with an additional J85 turbojet for landing, would have had a 48-ft-long expendable component powered by two Marquardt RJ-59 ramjets.

After release from the B-58 at Mach 2, the composite vehicle would have accelerated to Mach 4 and 91,000 ft, using all three ramjets to travel for a further 2950 miles. Having launched its atomic warhead-carrying burden, the 46-ft-long parasite aircraft would have then returned to its base, where the B-58A component should have already arrived home.

The 'Super Hustler's' lack of stealth characteristics led to an improved 'First Invisible Super Hustler' (FISH) study by Donald Kirk's team. It featured a smaller, one-man front section that included a jettisonable escape capsule, television cameras for forward vision and 'stealthy' wings with curved leading edges incorporating the dialectric radar-absorbent, wedge-shaped, inserts that were similar to the stealth-inducing structures used by Lockheed for the A-12. Dropped from a B-58, it would have used its two ramjets to carry out a similar mission to the original 'Super Hustler' composite.

Convair received the go-ahead to build the FISH in December 1958 after the CIA's consideration of Lockheed's non-stealthy, ramjet-powered Archangel 1 proposal. Initially, 12 FISH and three carrier B-58As, based at Carswell, were specified. Pre-production design and subcontracting work was started at Fort Worth, but wind tunnel tests soon revealed that the presence of the large FISH payload under a B-58 caused unacceptable drag, tripling its acceleration time to Mach 2. The FISH would also have needed the longer, more powerful B-58B to provide a suitable carrier, but when the advanced bomber failed to secure a production contract the FISH had to be abandoned too.

Design studies for a revised, hugely expensive 'KingFISH' project continued into 1960. It became a single-stage vehicle without a B-58 carrier, and was to be powered by two J58 turbojets as fitted to the A-12, which it began to resemble more closely on the drawing board. Reconnaissance variants that could have reached Mach 6 at 125,000 ft were also proposed by Convair, but Lockheed's design won the day in August 1959 and the 'Skunk Works' set about the detailed development of its A-12/SR-71 high-altitude, high-Mach reconnaissance aircraft.

The unusually large 40-inch diameter antenna of the AN/ASG-18 for the YF-12A. Note also the infra-red sensor domes fitted to either side of 55-0665's nose. When flight testing of the system ended in February 1964, 'Snoopy' was retired to the Edwards AFB photo test range and gradually reduced to a skeleton (*Terry Panopalis Collection*)

The A-12, later modified into the SR-71, also gave rise to Project *Kedlock* – the YF-12A intended for the long-range Mach 3 interceptor role that Convair had explored for a Hustler derivative in 1951 known as the B-58D. Eight years later, the YF-12A required a supersonic test-bed for its Hughes AN/ASG-18 fire-control system and GAR-9 (AIM-47A) missile, both of which had been developed for the cancelled F-108 Rapier. YB-58 55-0665, used for the USAF's Phase IV testing, was fitted with the AN/ASG-18's radar, including a massive 40-inch diameter antenna, in an extended radome that added seven feet to the aircraft's length. A pod was also designed to carry and launch a GAR-9.

The work had been completed by 2 August 1959, and 55-0665 flight-tested the system for two years from 1960, conducting a test-firing of the GAR-9 on 25 May 1962. The missile's long-range capability was proven in a launch against an airborne target at a range of 13 miles, and tests continued until the programme was ended in February 1964. In a later test using a YF-12A in September 1966, a GAR-9 launched at Mach 3.2 and 74,000 ft hit a target drone QB-47 flying at sea level.

The prospect of using the B-58 as an ALBM platform remained alive throughout 1958-60, and there was even a suggestion in 1960 to equip it with air-to-air missiles. As a stand-off missile carrier, the bomber would have had a markedly increased range. Lockheed duly began studying suitable missiles for the B-58, using parts from its existing weapons such as the Polaris and Sergeant missiles. The designs, one of them a reconnaissance vehicle, used a 50,000-lb thrust rocket motor to power a slender, 30-ft-long missile weighing around 12,000 lbs.

Faithful test-bed YB-58 55-0660 was used for the first test launch on 5 September 1958 at Mach 1 and 40,500 ft. Although the missile successfully blasted away from its centreline pylon, control problems terminated the flight early. The second 'High Virgo' example, painted bright red, made a successful flight, reaching Mach 6 at 250,000 ft on a 185-mile trajectory. Three more launches were made in mid-1959. The first of these ascended to 169,000 ft using its own inertial guidance system, and the second was intended to test a 13-camera installation in the missile's nose to photograph both the missile and an Explorer IV satellite. Following on from similar tests with a Martin Bold Orion ALBM launched from a B-47, this was the beginning of a programme to test the feasibility of destroying hostile or redundant satellites using a nuclear

This cine film still shows Lockheed ALBM 'King Lofus IV' being carried beneath XB-58 55-0660. The fourth and final ALBM trial with a Lockheed missile was conducted on 22 September 1959, and like the previous three launches, it was only partially successful. The project was terminated shortly afterwards (*Terry Panopalis Collection*)

warhead if necessary. The third launch was abandoned due to faulty data on the satellite's orbital pattern, and a final attempt on 22 September used the Explorer V satellite as a 'target'. An apparently successful mission was curtailed by loss of communication with the 'King Lofus IV' High Virgo ALBM, the missile's camera package never being found.

The anti-satellite (ASAT) concept was revived in 1982 and a Vought ASM-135 ASAT missile was launched from an F-15 Eagle in September 1985 against the US Solwind P78-1 satellite. Thereafter, ground-launched missiles were seen as a more effective method of dealing with errant satellites, although Project *Close Shot* envisaged a B-52 launching a missile to place an object such as a small satellite in orbit.

A B-58 carried another type of passenger in July 1959 when 55-0662 was modified to convey a pod containing a GE J93-GE-3 engine – the intended turbojet for North American's XB-70 and F-108. Weighing 6000 lbs, the 20-ft-long engine developed 31,500 lbs of thrust and introduced air-cooled titanium turbine blades. Bearing its massive engine pod, the YB-58, now with the equivalent power of six J79s, made several flights as an NB-58A in 1959, reaching Mach 2 without having to use full power on all of its own engines. This programme was ended when funding for the two North American aircraft ran out and 55-0662 was restored to its normal YB-58 configuration. The jet then became a TB-58A, and it served as the chase aircraft for the XB-70 test programme.

TO THE DESERT

From 1959 onwards US defence strategy began to move away from the all-nuclear bomber concept and embrace conventional munitions capability or lower-yield atomic weapons for what were seen as limited wars. TAC under Gen Frank Everest began to evaluate a wide range of ordnance for its tactical nuclear strike aircraft, while SAC adapted some aircraft for non-nuclear operations while preserving its primary nuclear posture. Three B-47 wings could carry conventional weapons, including up to 25 1000-lb bombs internally, and converting the B-52D into the 'bomb truck' configuration, with 108 bombs (which it would adopt for Vietnam), was comparatively straightforward. Clearly the B-58A with its single weapons pod and limited external pylons for nuclear stores was at a disadvantage in that context, and this became a factor in its rapid demise.

The projected B-58E, with twin engines and conventional weapons loads like those trialled in Operation *Bullseye*, was briefly a rival for the Tactical Fighter Experimental programme that culminated in the creation of the F-111. However, the B-58's fuel-filled wings would have made it very susceptible to AAA damage if it had been used in a tactical role. Although 'Vietnam camouflage' drawings were issued for the Hustler, implying that it might be used in that conflict, its susceptibility to AAA and lack of a substantial conventional bombload effectively ruled out a combat role for the jet in the eyes of SAC planners. Also, they were already risking a considerable part of their B-52 alert force in Vietnam, and the idea of SIOP B-58As being put at risk by flying through North Vietnam's highly effective air defence network was clearly insupportable.

In 1972, near-supersonic low-altitude attacks against targets in North Vietnam by solo TAC F-111As – fitted with the terrain-following radar that the B-58A lacked – were actually very effective. SAC's FB-111A (which partially replaced the B-58A from 1968 and adopted SIOP duties from 1971) in turn became an interim purchase pending the eventual acquisition of the Rockwell B-1B Lancer. The latter was a more potent replacement for the Hustler, despite its much lower Mach 1.25 maximum speed at altitude.

UNFAIR DISMISSAL?

Although Defense Secretary Robert S McNamara had little interest in a direct replacement for the maligned B-58A when, as he planned, it was to be retired in 1965, he nevertheless asked the USAF for suggestions in 1963. Gen Tom Power, SAC's commanding general, requested the reactivation of B-58A production, describing the bomber as 'One of the finest weapon systems in the world'. It was a sentiment loudly endorsed by most crews who flew the Hustler. Unimpressed, McNamara adhered to the original production limit of 116 B-58s – the smallest number of any type of bomber supplied to the USA from 1936 to 1962 – although he also extended the retirement date to 1971 without consulting the Joint Chiefs of Staff.

On 29 October 1969 new Defense Secretary Melvin Laird perpetuated LeMay's hostile stance towards the aircraft and preference for large, heavy bombers. He announced that the Hustler would be retired from 31 January 1970, four years earlier than in SAC's original plans, after only eight years of frontline service. He cited the need for budget cuts and the redundancy of high-altitude nuclear strike capability against a far better-defended Communist bloc. Four wings of B-52C/Fs would continue in service instead, and they would be required to maintain the nuclear deterrent (needing at least 170 B-52s) while a large part of the nuclear B-52G force was occupied in Vietnam.

Laird's decision was no doubt influenced by the negative views that Maj Gen Glen W Martin, USAF Director of Plans, expressed to USAF Chief of Staff, Gen John D Ryan, on the B-58s' worth compared with retaining four wings of B-52s. The Commander-in-Chief of SAC, Gen Bruce Holloway, concurred with Martin, while Pentagon advisors on the B-58 were not consulted.

The aircraft's proven value as a low-level intruder that left most contemporary interceptors standing and had a much better chance of evading enemy radars was not mentioned, neither was the much higher structural toll inflicted on B-52 airframes when they were re-purposed as low-altitude attackers. Operational use had shown that the B-58A could sustain 700 mph at altitudes below 500 ft and still give a stable ride, allowing accurate bomb delivery even without terrain-following radar. Many strategists felt that the Soviet Union regarded the Hustler as a major threat, in much the same way as it viewed the F-111 a decade later, and the sacrifice of the B-58 force was a factor in securing agreement at the Strategic Arms Limitation Talks that began in November 1969.

SAC was allowed a three-month period to wind down its B-58 operations, but many problems had already arisen due to lack of spare parts, rising maintenance costs and airframe fatigue due to the small fleet's high total of flying hours. To USAF accountants, Hustlers had been more than three times as expensive as B-52s to buy (partly due to the small production run), and it was claimed that they were also three times as costly to operate. However, figures produced by the Pentagon's Plans Division showed this to be untrue. In fact, it could be argued that the use of only two B-58 bases with smaller units and less tanking requirements than the B-52 made the Hustler slightly cheaper to operate overall than the Stratofortress. Ironically, the early B-52s for which the B-58 was sacrificed were themselves withdrawn from service in the late 1960s.

A high accident rate was cited as another reason for early B-58 withdrawal, including the assertion that there had been 26 losses. In reality, only 17 had been lost after USAF service began, two of them at the Paris Airshow, and the overall loss rate could be calculated at 1.4 annually over ten years of service – a figure that was less than many other more docile USAF types.

At Little Rock AFB, DSO Dick Dirga and his colleagues were shocked to read in their local paper in October 1969 that all Hustlers were to be withdrawn. The crews were dispersed within a month, with many pilots going to Vietnam to fly other types, while navigators were reassigned to B-52 or FB-111A units and many DSOs ended up in the KC-135A tankers that had previously refuelled their Hustlers.

Some aviators, including Operation *Heat Rise* pilot Maj Robert 'Gray' Sowers, had already joined the initial cadre of *Senior Crown* SR-71 crews who came from SAC bomber and U-2 units. Half of the initial 26 crewmen assigned to the SR-71-equipped 9th Strategic Reconnaissance Wing (SRW) came directly from the B-58A. Sowers put his Mach 2 Hustler experience to good use as the first SR-71 instructor pilot, surviving a 1968 ejection from an SR-71B. Lt Col Confer, the second USAF pilot to fly the Hustler, also moved to the SR-71 as a Test and Evaluation pilot, and in 1970 he became commander of the 9th SRW.

B-58A 59-2446 from the 43rd BW was the first Hustler to head for the Military Aircraft Storage and Disposition Center (MASDC) at Davis-Monthan AFB on 5 November 1969, and the 305th BW sent its last two examples – early TB-58A 55-0662 and late-production B-58A 61-2078 *Top Dawg* – on 16 January 1970. The last aircraft to pass through General Dynamics' Waco, Texas, 'Hustle-Up' modification line was sent directly into storage at Davis-Monthan, where it joined rows of other redundant Hustlers. By 1979 they had all been scrapped, apart from a few notable record-breakers that went to museums.

To preserve their historical lineage, the two Hustler wings were re-designated, the 43rd BW becoming the 43rd Strategic Wing at Andersen AFB, equipped with B-52s, and the 305th BW converted to KC-135As and EC-135Cs as the 305th Air Refuelling Wing, remaining at Grissom AFB.

APPENDICES

COLOUR PLATES

1
XB-58-CF 55-0660, Convair plant, Fort Worth, Texas, November 1956

Later re-designated YB/RB-58, 55-0660 (the prototype Hustler) first flew on 11 November 1956 and went on to complete 257.5 hours of test flights, including the type's first Mach 1 and Mach 2 tests. An initial scheme including white under the fuselage was replaced by the distinctive red and white colours used on the first four aircraft. Early flights were made without a pod, although the aircraft is depicted here with an MB-1 in place. 55-0660 continued test flying until April 1960, participating in a fuel management programme and ALBM carriage trials. Transferred to Kelly AFB, Texas, for ground-instructional training, it was unceremoniously scrapped there shortly after its arrival.

2
TB-58A-CF 55-0661 *MACH-IN-BOID* of the 305th BW, Bunker Hill AFB, Indiana, 1964

The second YB/RB-58, which first flew on 16 February 1957, subsequently completed the first test flight with a pod attached. In a full career, the jet performed Phase II flight testing prior to being transferred to the 6592nd TS. With this unit it undertook low-altitude ejection seat trials, in-flight refuelling proving flights and live downward-ejection seat tests using a modified MB-1 pod fitted with experimental seats in February 1962. Converted to TB-58A configuration as part of the second batch of four trainers, ordered in October 1960, it was issued to the 305th BW. The wing retained the Hustler's *MACH-IN-BOID* nickname just forward of the cockpit, the jet having worn this sobriquet when adorned in a red and white scheme during its time as a trials aircraft. 55-0661 was retired to MASDC in September 1970 and scrapped in July 1977.

3
YB-58-CF 55-0662 of the 6592nd TS, Carswell AFB, March 1959

This aircraft's very full test programme included the first drop of a pod (in May 1957), flight-testing of the navigation/bombing suite and autopilot, including the radar altimeter and Doppler radar, and tests of frangible undercarriage wheels. In a further revision, the Hustler became a TB-58A and contributed to the XB-70 Valkyrie's development by performing the role of chase aircraft for most of its test flights from September 1965. 55-0662 then moved to the 305th BW as a crew trainer, completing a record 256 faultless sorties. Flown to MASDC in January 1970, the aircraft was scrapped in July 1970.

4
NB-58A-CF 55-0662 of ARDC, Edwards AFB, California, September 1959

As an NB-58A, 55-0662 also became the flight test-bed for the GE J93 turbojet destined to power the XB-70A Valkyrie bomber and F-108 Rapier fighter. Modifications to the aircraft's fuel system and instrumentation by GE and Convair allowed the Hustler to use its own engines together with the centreline pod-mounted YJ93-GE-3 to develop the equivalent power of six J79 engines for Mach 2 test flights. When the programme was curtailed by defence budget shrinkage and cancellation of XB-70/F-108 research, 55-0662 was converted into a TB-58A trainer as part of the second batch of Hustlers to be modified.

5
YB-58-CF 55-0663 of the 6592nd TS, Kirtland AFB, New Mexico, October 1957

The fourth B-58 built, this aircraft was vital to the pod development process, performing the first MB-1 supersonic drop on 30 September 1957 followed by the first at Mach 2 two months later. In 1960 55-0663 also dropped both sections of the TCP for the first time. Seconded to NASA, the aircraft took part in its research into sonic booms in 1962 before undergoing conversion into a TB-58A for the 305th BW. After a cockpit fire caused by ignition of an oxygen leak ended its flying days in 1969, the aircraft was superficially repaired and then put on display as a gate guardian at Grissom AFB. 55-0662 was moved to Grissom Air Museum, near Peru, Indiana, in 1982, where it remains on display today.

6
YB-58-CF 55-0665, Hughes Aircraft Company, Culver City, California, August 1959

As the first B-58 to be delivered to the USAF for Phase IV acceptance testing in February 1958, this aircraft was converted into a test-bed for the Hughes AN/ASG-18 fire control system and GAR-9 air-to-air missile the following year. Saved from the abandoned F-108 programme, the AN/ASG-18 was intended for the YF-12A interceptor. An extended radome, adding more than seven feet to the aircraft's length, covered the system's 40-inch-diameter radar dish, while the GAR-9 (AIM-47A) was housed in a newly-designed pod from which the missile was fired via an internal trapeze-type launcher. After flight-testing up to 1963, it was clear that the programme could be continued with the YF-12A itself, and the final launches from 55-0665 (nicknamed 'Snoopy') occurred in February 1964. The programme was then terminated and the Hustler dumped on the photo test-range at Edwards AFB, where it was progressively taken apart.

7
TB-58A-CF 55-0670, Convair plant, Fort Worth, Texas, May 1960

Built as a YB/RB-58A, this aircraft was used by the 6592nd TS as the climatic test airframe within the extreme temperature test chamber at Eglin AFB (where it was housed between July and September 1958), followed by realistic conditions at Eielson AFB, Alaska. For those tests it was equipped with versions of operational equipment, including the tail gun installation. 55-0670 then entered Convair's rework line on 5 October 1959 for conversion as the prototype TB-58A. It emerged on 10 May 1960 for its first flight of 1 hr 40 min, crewed by Val Prahl, Earl Guthrie and Grover Tate, before delivery to the 43rd BW in August in a rather less spectacular colour scheme. It served there until withdrawal in December 1969 and scrapping in August 1977.

8
B-58A-10-CF 58-1007 *Super Sue*, Convair plant, Fort Worth, Texas, 1959

Built as a YB/RB-58A, 58-1007 was the 14th Hustler completed by Convair. First flown on 8 November 1958, it was used by the company as a test-bed for the six sub-systems of the Sperry Gyroscope Corporation AN/ASQ-42 navigation/bombing equipment. It was then converted into a TB-58A for use by the 43rd BW (*see* Colour Plate 9).

9
TB-58A-10-CF 58-1007 *BOOMERANG* of the 43rd BW, Carswell AFB, Texas, 1962

58-1007 became the third TB-58A, replacing 55-0669 (which was destroyed in a crash before conversion to trainer configuration) in the original batch of four Hustler trainers. Depicted here with a TCP upper component, the aircraft was assigned to the 43rd BW. Retirement to MASDC occurred on 15 January 1977 and Southwestern Alloys of Tucson, Arizona, reduced the Hustler to scrap on 5 August 1977.

10
YB/RB-58A-10-CF 58-1009 *BONANZA* of the 6592nd TS, Edwards AFB, California, 1959

The 16th Hustler built (hence its original *Sweet Sixteen* nickname), this aircraft first flew on 15 December 1958 and participated in tests of the complex fuel system and the AN/ASQ-42 navigation/ bombing system with the 6592nd TS. It was the fourth aircraft to be updated for service use as a B-58A with the 43rd BW. Retired to MASDC in December 1969, the bomber was scrapped in July 1977.

11
B-58A-10-CF 58-1015 *"Ginger"* of ARDC, Edwards AFB, California, 1960

After its first flight on 19 March 1959, this aircraft (the 22nd Hustler built) was used for pod drop tests (it has a TCP upper component here) and low-level flights as *Little Joe* to prove the aircraft's capability as a nuclear penetrator. On 15 October 1959 it made the B-58's first sustained flight at Mach 2 during a 1 hr 10 min journey from Seattle to Dallas. After repairs to damage sustained in a landing with burst main gear tyres at Edwards AFB on 13 April 1960, 58-1015 became the last Hustler to pass through the conversion re-work programme that upgraded pre-production jets to production standard for the 43rd BW. The wing took delivery of the bomber on 25 October 1962. Retired to MASDC in December 1969, 58-1015 was scrapped in July 1977.

12
B-58A-10-CF 58-1011 *'THE PULASKI HUSTLER'* of the 43rd BW, Little Rock AFB, Arkansas, September 1964

First flown on 30 January 1959, this aircraft subsequently made the first pod drop using a fully operational AN/ASQ-42 system. It later entered the production conversion programme and was delivered to the 43rd BW at Little Rock AFB in August 1964, where the jet carried the nicknames *'THE PULASKI HUSTLER'* (later switched to 59-2429), *Wicked Witch* and the more appropriate *Trail Blazer*. Depicted here with the two-component pod, 58-1011 was flown to MASDC on 11 December 1969 and scrapped in June 1977.

13
B-58A-10-CF 58-1016 *CHAMPION OF CHAMPIONS* of the 43rd BW, Carswell AFB, Texas, 1963

In 1960 this aircraft featured in a USAF-sponsored promotional film presented by actor and USAF Reserve officer Brig Gen James Stewart (a former B-24 Liberator pilot) to emphasise the B-58's range and low-altitude penetration capability. During the film's production Stewart made a Mach 2 flight in a TB-58A flown by Maj John Irving. The Hustler's five speed-related trophies and success in breaking 14 world records by that time were also celebrated in the film, and in the aircraft's nickname. 58-1016 was lost after a heavy landing at Little Rock AFB on 20 May 1965. Although pilot Capt Ralph L Semann and DSO Maj Vincent Karaba survived, navigator Capt Steve Kirchler Jr was killed.

14
YB/RB-58A-10-CF 58-1018 *REDDY KILOWATT* of the 6592nd TS, Edwards AFB, 1961

First flown on 29 April 1959 as the 25th Hustler built, 58-1018 tested the AN/ALR-12 radar warning system, AN/ALQ-16 radar track breaker and AN/ALE-16 chaff dispensers. Its left main landing gear partially failed on take-off from Edwards AFB at the start of a test flight on 19 September 1961, although the bomber was recovered successfully. 58-1018 became the eighth Hustler to enter the production conversion programme, after which it was operated by the 43rd BW with the nickname *Omega*. The jet was scrapped in June 1977.

15
B-58A-10-CF 59-2428 *BEN-HUR* of the 43rd BW, Carswell AFB, Texas, 1960

This was the first tactical inventory Hustler to be delivered to the 6592nd TS and the first to include a service standard M61A1 tail gun installation. Its pre-squadron service period included cold weather testing at Ellsworth AFB, South Dakota, in January 1960's Project *White Horse*. In January 1963 59-2428 was the first B-58 to enter the Phase I 'Hustle-Up' modernisation programme and also the first to complete Phase II. It was then reissued to the 43rd BW. Here, the bomber carries a TCP. Transferred to MASDC in January 1970, the bomber was scrapped in July 1977.

16
B-58A-10-CF 59-2431 of the 6592nd TS, Edwards AFB, California, 1960

This was the fourth production-configured B-58A, and it is seen here in the markings of the 6592nd TS that includes an early version of the standard anti-dazzle paint ahead of the windscreen. The squadron, managed by ARDC, included both pre-production and production-standard Hustlers within its ranks from January 1958 through to August 1960. While with this unit, 59-2431 undertook a flight that included 78 minutes spent at Mach 2. Subsequently issued to the 43rd BW, the jet remained with the wing until flown to the MASDC in December 1969. It was scrapped in June 1977.

17
B-58A-10-CF 59-2434 *CANNONBALL* of the 43rd BW, Carswell AFB, Texas, 1961

Seen in standard SAC markings, 59-2434 was the first B-58 to enter the 1960 *Flash-Up* programme aimed at standardising service Hustlers and ensuring commonality to eliminate anomalies in their maintenance procedures. The 43rd BW had been an SAC training wing for some time, making it an ideal organisation to introduce the B-58 operationally. *CANNONBALL* remained in service until December 1969, when it was delivered to MASDC. Like a number of stored Hustlers, the bomber was scrapped in June 1977.

18
B-58A-10-CF 59-2435 *SHACKBUSTER* of the 43rd BW, Kirtland AFB, New Mexico, October 1961

This hard-working Hustler was a vital element in the pod-drop programme that began at Kirtland AFB (where the Sandia Corporation designed the TX-53 nuclear warhead for carriage by the B-58) in November 1957, making the first Mach 2 drop of the upper component of a TCP on 10 February 1961 and following up with a Mach 2 lower component delivery on 8 August. YB-58 55-0663 was also used. In all, 59-2435 made 17 TCP test drops, as well as releasing numerous B43 nuclear shapes from external pylons. These were all meticulously recorded in the form of 17 instrumented pod-drop markings and 40 bomb symbols painted below the cockpit. Delivered to MASDC in July 1970, this aircraft was also scrapped in June 1977.

19
B-58A-10-CF 59-2438 of the 43rd BW, Carswell AFB, Texas, 1963

This aircraft is depicted carrying an LA-1 reconnaissance pod, which had its camera located in the lower nose area of the external store. Aside from occasional use by 59-2438, the LA-1 was also carried by several other suitably modified Hustlers within the 43rd BW. 59-2438's relatively plain markings are typical of most SAC-operated B-58As. This example was sent to MASDC in December 1969 and scrapped in May 1977.

20
B-58A-10-CF 59-2442 of the 43rd BW, Carswell AFB, Texas, 1961

This aircraft (with 59-2441 *Road Runner*) was used for Project *Quick Step I* at Edwards AFB in January 1961 when six speed-with-payload world records were beaten. Nicknamed *Untouchable* at the time, this aircraft set three records on 12 January, completing the course with minimal fuel reserves. It was followed by *Road Runner*'s three records 48 hours later that earned the latter's crew the Thompson Trophy. With the 43rd BW, 59-2442 was equipped to carry an LA-1 pod, as depicted here. It was the last B-58 to leave Little Rock AFB in December 1969 for disposal at MASDC, where it was scrapped in September 1977.

21
B-58A-10-CF 59-2447 *RAPID RABBIT* of the 43rd BW, Carswell AFB, Texas, 1961

59-2447 became the second operational B-58 loss after it had a terminal failure in its Mach trim control system at high speed near Lawton, Oklahoma, on 15 February 1962. The crew, Maj John Irving and Capts John Fuller and Don Avallon, ejected successfully with the aircraft in an inverted spin.

22
B-58A-10-CF 59-2451 *The Firefly* of the 43rd BW, Le Bourget, France, June 1961

Famous for its 26 May 1961 world record flight from New York to Paris in 3 hrs 19 min 51 sec, averaging 1089.36 mph and winning the McKay and Harmon Trophies, *The Firefly* had already set a world speed record on 10 May. Over a closed circuit 666-mile course, Majs Elmer E Murphy and Eugene F Moses and 1Lt David F Dickerson, all from the 65th BS, averaged 1302.07 mph for more than 30 minutes and became outright winners of the Blériot Trophy. After its Paris appearance, for which the red tail stripes were added, the aircraft and the same crew were lost in a crash shortly after take-off from Le Bourget on 3 June 1961.

23
B-58A-20-CF 61-2053 of the 305th BW, Bunker Hill AFB, Indiana, 1967

Assigned to the 305th BW in the late 1960s and armed with a two-component pod, this Hustler displays its wing's membership of the Second Air Force with a winged '2' tail motif. Although not visible in this artwork, the jet had its 'last three' (053) in red on the nose-gear doors, together with the crew names Capt Kiepe (pilot), Capt Klingbiel (navigator) and Capt Phail (DSO). It was flown to MASDC on 6 January 1970 and scrapped in July 1977.

24
B-58A-10-CF 59-2458 *STAR RAKER* of the 43rd BW, Carswell AFB, Texas, March 1962

Winner of the Bendix and McKay Trophies for Capts Robert 'Gray' Sowers, Robert MacDonald and John Walton, this aircraft beat speed records set by an F4H-1 Phantom II and RF-101 Voodoo during the course of its Operation *Heat Rise* record flight from Los Angeles to New York and back again on 5 March 1962. Specially waxed and polished for the flight, the B-58 was otherwise a standard operational Hustler. The aircraft reached a speed of 1400 mph during *Heat Rise*, at which point skin temperature approached the critical 125°C level at which the aluminium honeycomb panels could start to delaminate. Most of the jet's decal markings were burned off during the flight. Also nicknamed *The Cowtown Hustler*, 59-2458 was retired in December 1969 and later put on permanent display at the National Museum of the USAF at Wright-Patterson AFB.

25
B-58A-10-CF 59-2461 *HOOSIER HUSTLER* of the 305th BW, Bunker Hill AFB, Indiana, 11 May 1961

Initially assigned to the 43rd BW, this aircraft became the first Hustler for the 305th BW on 11 May 1961. At its new Bunker Hill AFB it adopted a popular nickname for the residents of the state of Indiana, 'Hoosiers'. It was later re-marked to resemble 59-2451 for a film about *The Firefly*'s record flight. The bomber was sent to MASDC in January 1970 and scrapped there in August 1977.

26
B-58A-20-CF 61-2059 *GREASED LIGHTNING* of the 305th BW, Bunker Hill AFB, Indiana, October 1963

The last in a long series of official record-setting flights for the B-58 was undertaken by Majs Sidney Kubesch and John Barrett and Capt Gerard Williamson on 16 October 1963. On a non-stop supersonic flight starting from Kadena AB, Okinawa, and ending at RAF Greenham Common, England (but measured from Tokyo to London), *GREASED LIGHTNING* recorded five hours at between 950 knots and 1230 knots until a faulty afterburner encountered after its fifth aerial refuelling reduced the overall average to 812 knots. Following its withdrawal from service, the aircraft was displayed at Offutt AFB's SAC Museum in Belleville, Nebraska.

27
B-58A-20-CF 61-2066 of the 43rd BW, Carswell AFB, Texas, 1968

This aircraft was used for test work by Convair prior to it being issued to the 43rd BW, the Hustler being equipped for four 2100-lb B43 Class D nuclear bombs on detachable external pylons, which were tested with other conventional armament at Kirtland AFB in 1961 and installed on all B-58s from the 87th jet (61-2051) onwards. 61-2066, the 102nd Hustler built, was sent to MASDC in January 1970 and was scrapped there in June 1977.

28
B-58A-20-CF 61-2068 *DEPUTY DAWG* of the 305th BW, Bunker Hill AFB, Indiana, 1967

Markings on B-58s in squadron service were restrained and limited to the SAC sash and shield, incorporating the bomb wing patch on the right side of the nose. Nicknames were also seen on about 40 examples, and they were changed periodically depending on the preferences of ground- and aircrews. *DEPUTY DAWG* served at Grissom AFB until its withdrawal in December 1969. It was also scrapped at MASDC in June 1977.

29
B-58A-20-CF 61-2060 of the 305th BW, Bunker Hill AFB, Indiana, 1967

In basic, standardised SAC markings, this aircraft carries a twin-component, 54-ft-long pod that was released from its pylon by a 'kicker' device installed in a fin at the tail-end of the lower pod component. After release, the upper component split in two as it approached its target and jettisoned its fuel sections and other equipment that the warhead did not require. This aircraft was withdrawn from service at Grissom AFB in December 1969 and scrapped in August 1977.

30
B-58A-10-CF 59-2447 of the 43rd BW in (potential) Vietnam War camouflage, Southeast Asia, late 1960s

This 'what if' profile assumes that B-58A 59-2447 had survived to join a deployment to a base in Thailand to conduct strike missions against North Vietnam in the late 1960s. A version of SAC's B-52G TO 1-1-4 Vietnam camouflage scheme was officially designed for the B-58, and radar targets and offsets were allegedly established in case a deployment was approved. There is no evidence that such a scheme was ever actually applied to a B-58.

At the end of their relatively short USAF careers, more than 80 B-58s had been consigned to MASDC at Davis-Monthan AFB by January 1971 for eventual scrapping by Southwestern Alloys of Tucson, Arizona, in 1977-78. Six were saved for museum displays and two stood derelict – 59-2437 *Firefly 2* at Little Rock AFB (later restored at Lackland AFB, Texas) and the remains of 'Snoopy' at Edwards AFB (*Terry Panopalis Collection*)

INDEX

Page numbers in **bold** refer to figures. Plate numbers are **bold** followed by the page number and caption locater in brackets.